CONTENTS

2   The Four Operations of Decimals

BLANK

EXERCISE 1

1. Write each fraction as a decimal.

(a)

2 tenths

$\dfrac{2}{10} =$

(b)

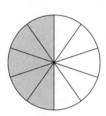

5 tenths

$\dfrac{5}{10} =$

(c)

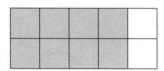

8 tenths

$\dfrac{8}{10} =$

(d)

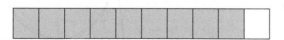

9 tenths

$\dfrac{9}{10} =$

2. What is the amount of water in liters?
   Give the answer as a decimal.

(a)

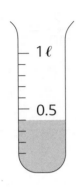

_____ ℓ

(b)

_____ ℓ

3. What is the weight in kilograms?
   Give the answer as a decimal.

(a)

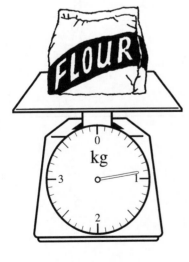

_____ kg

(b)

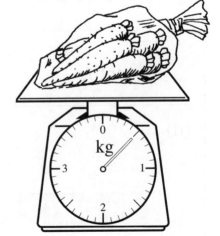

_____ kg

4. Write a decimal for each of the following:

(a)

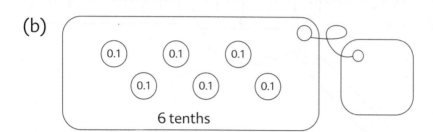

2 tenths

(b)

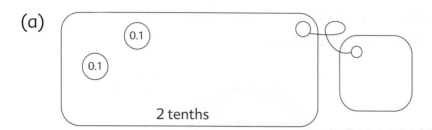

6 tenths

(c)

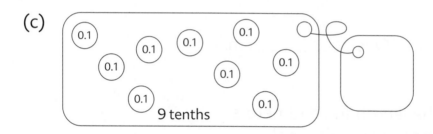

9 tenths

5. Write the missing number in each of the following:

(a)

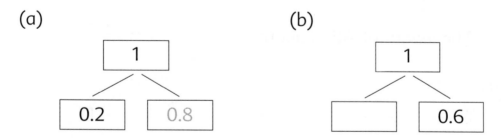

(b)

(c)

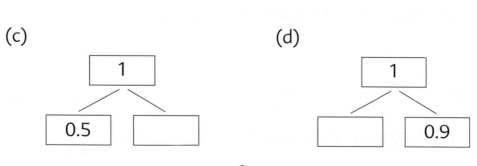

(d)

EXERCISE 2

1. What is the length of PQ in centimeters?
   Give the answer as a decimal.

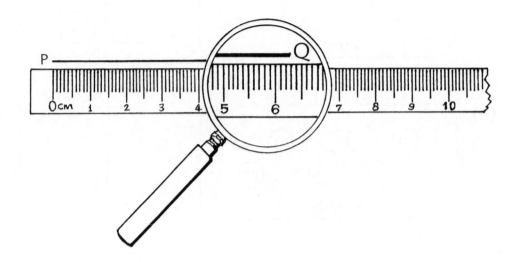

   The length of PQ is _____ cm.

2. Measure the length in centimeters.
   Give the answer as a decimal.

   (a)

   A ———————————————— B

   The length of AB is about _____ cm.

   (b)

   C ——————————————————— D

   The length of CD is about _____ cm.

   (c)

   E ——————————————— F

   The length of EF is about _____ cm.

3. What is the amount of water in liters?
   Give the answer as a decimal.

(a)

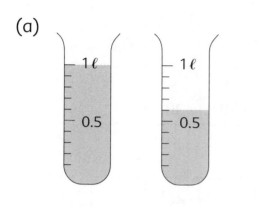

_____ ℓ

(b)

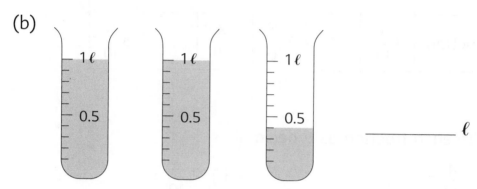

_____ ℓ

4. What is the weight in kilograms?
   Give the answer as a decimal.

(a)   (b)

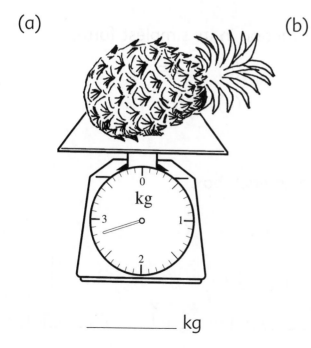   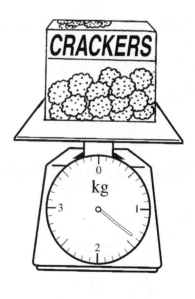

_____ kg   _____ kg

EXERCISE 3

1. Complete the following tables.

Decimal	0.1	0.2				0.6
Fraction	$\dfrac{1}{10}$		$\dfrac{3}{10}$	$\dfrac{4}{10}$	$\dfrac{5}{10}$	

Decimal	1.1	1.2			2.2	
Fraction	$1\dfrac{1}{10}$		$1\dfrac{3}{10}$	$1\dfrac{4}{10}$		$3\dfrac{5}{10}$

2. Write each fraction as a decimal.

   (a) $\dfrac{4}{10} =$ (b) $1\dfrac{4}{10} =$

   (c) $\dfrac{5}{10} =$ (d) $3\dfrac{5}{10} =$

3. Write each decimal as a fraction in its simplest form.

   (a) 0.3 =   (b) 2.3 =

   (c) 0.6 =   (d) 3.6 =

4. Write the missing decimal in each box.

   (a)

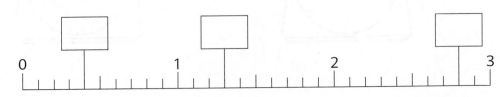

12

(b)

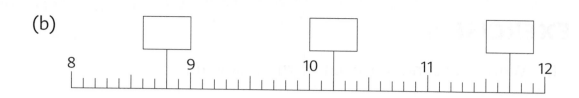

(c)

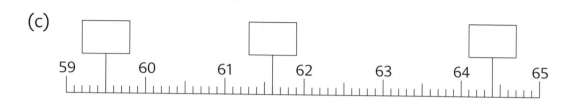

5. Write **>** (is greater than), **<** (is less than) or **=** (is equal to) in each ☐.

(a) 6.0 ☐ $\frac{6}{10}$ (b) 1 ☐ 0.1

(c) 2.0 ☐ 2   (d) 5 ☐ 3.8

6. Circle the smallest number in each set.

(a) 3.1, 0.1, 0.3, 1.3

(b) 0.9, 1.9, 9, 9.1

7. Circle the greatest number in each set.

(a) 4.2, 3.2, 1.2, 6.2

(b) 2.1, 2.9, 2, 2.4

8. Complete the following number patterns.

(a) 2.1, 2.3, 2.5, _____, _____, 3.1

(b) 4.5, 5, 5.5, _____, _____, 7

13

EXERCISE 4

1. Write a decimal for each of the following:

(a)

Tens	Ones	Tenths
(10) (10) (10)	(1) (1) (1) (1)	(0.1) (0.1) (0.1) (0.1) (0.1) (0.1)

$30 + 4 + 0.6 =$

(b)

Tens	Ones	Tenths
(10) (10) (10) (10) (10)		(0.1) (0.1) (0.1) (0.1) (0.1) (0.1) (0.1)

$50 + 0.7 =$

(c)

Tens	Ones	Tenths
(10) (10) (10) (10)	(1) (1) (1) (1) (1)	(0.1) (0.1) (0.1)

$40 + 5 + 0.3 =$

(d)

Tens	Ones	Tenths
(10) (10) (10) (10)		(0.1) (0.1) (0.1) (0.1) (0.1) (0.1) (0.1) (0.1) (0.1)

$40 + 0.9 =$

2. Write the missing number in each box.

(a) $45.8 = 40 + 5 + \boxed{}$

(b) $70.3 = 70 + \boxed{}$

(c) $92.4 = \boxed{} + 2 + 0.4$

(d) $30.7 = \boxed{} + 0.7$

(e) $16.5 = 10 + 6 + \dfrac{\boxed{}}{10}$

(f) $60.9 = 60 + \dfrac{\boxed{}}{10}$

3. There are 12 pairs of equivalent numbers below. Circle each pair. (An example is shown.)

2.1	1.2	$\frac{2}{10}$	$1\frac{5}{10}$	5
0.1	$2\frac{1}{10}$	$1\frac{2}{10}$	0.5	1.5
0.3	$\frac{9}{10}$	0.9	$\frac{5}{10}$	0.8
$1\frac{3}{10}$	4.1	$4\frac{1}{10}$	$2\frac{8}{10}$	$3\frac{7}{10}$
1.3	$\frac{4}{10}$	2.8	3.7	6
0.4	1.4	$1\frac{4}{10}$	$\frac{6}{10}$	0.6

EXERCISE 5

1. Write the number represented by each of the following sets of number discs.

(a)

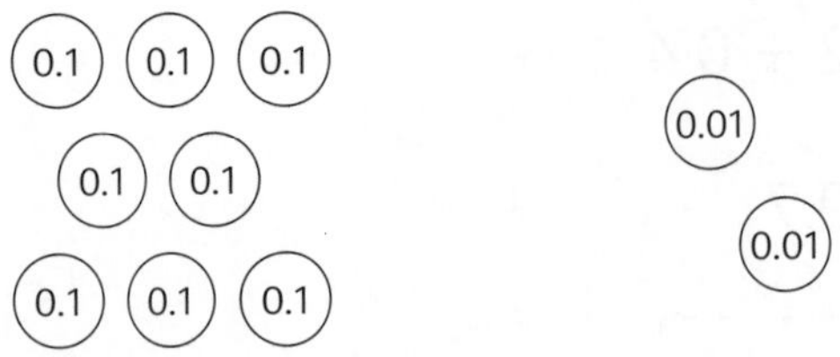

(b)

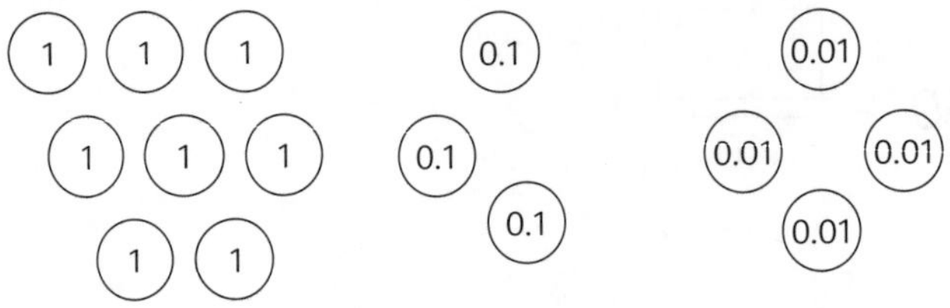

(c)

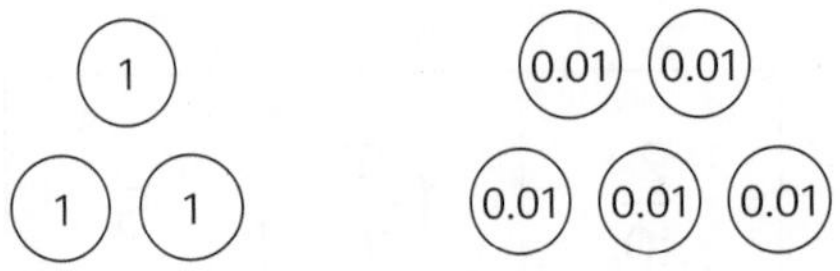

(d)

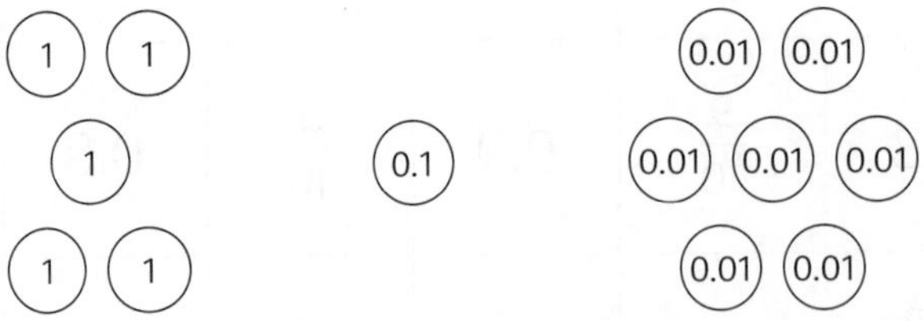

(e)

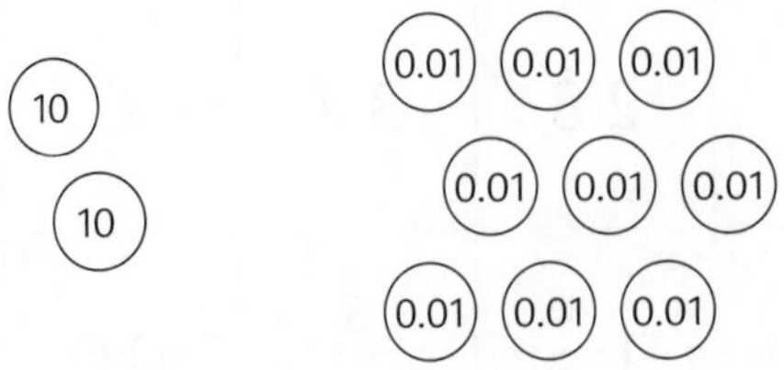

2. Write a decimal for each of the following:

(a)

Tens	Ones	Tenths	Hundredths
(10) (10) (10)	(1) (1) (1) (1)		(0.01) (0.01)

$30 + 4 + 0.02 =$

(b)

Tens	Ones	Tenths	Hundredths
(10) (10) (10) (10)		(0.1) (0.1)	(0.01) (0.01) (0.01) (0.01) (0.01)

$40 + 0.2 + 0.05 =$

(c)

Tens	Ones	Tenths	Hundredths
(10) (10)	(1) (1) (1) (1)	(0.1)	(0.01) (0.01) (0.01)

$20 + 4 + 0.1 + 0.03 =$

(d)

Tens	Ones	Tenths	Hundredths
(10) (10) (10)			(0.01) (0.01) (0.01) (0.01)

$30 + 0.04 =$

17

3. Fill in the blanks.

   (a) In 71.06, the digit _____ is in the tenths place.

      Its value is _____.

   (b) In 103.4, the digit _____ is in the tens place.

      Its value is _____.

   (c) In 19.4, the digit 4 is in the _____ place.

      Its value is _____.

   (d) In 57.01, the digit 5 is in the _____ place.

      Its value is _____.

   (e) In 28.63, the digit 3 is in the _____ place.

      Its value is _____.

   (f) In 90.72, the digit 0 is in the _____ place.

      Its value is _____.

4. Write the values of the digits in each of the following numbers.

   (a) 90.23

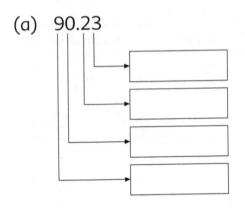

   (b) 87.41

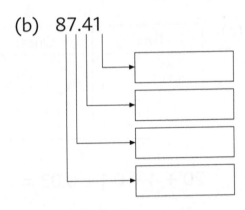

   (c) 56.09

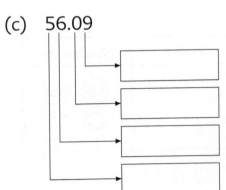

   (d) 218.8

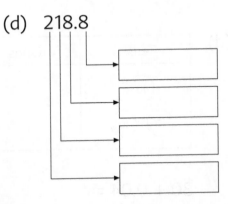

EXERCISE 6

1. Write each fraction as a decimal.

(a) 7 hundredths $\dfrac{7}{100} =$	(b) 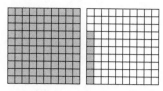 1 whole 7 hundredths $1\dfrac{7}{100} =$
(c) 58 hundredths $\dfrac{58}{100} =$	(d) 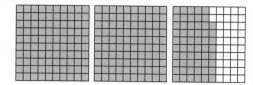 2 wholes 58 hundredths $2\dfrac{58}{100} =$
(e) $\dfrac{24}{100} =$	(f) $1\dfrac{24}{100} =$
(g) $\dfrac{65}{100} =$	(h) $3\dfrac{65}{100} =$
(i) $\dfrac{3}{100} =$	(j) $2\dfrac{3}{100} =$
(k) $\dfrac{5}{100} =$	(l) $10\dfrac{5}{100} =$

2. Join each fraction to its equivalent decimal with a straight line.
   (An example is shown.)
   If you do it correctly, you will get 3 squares.

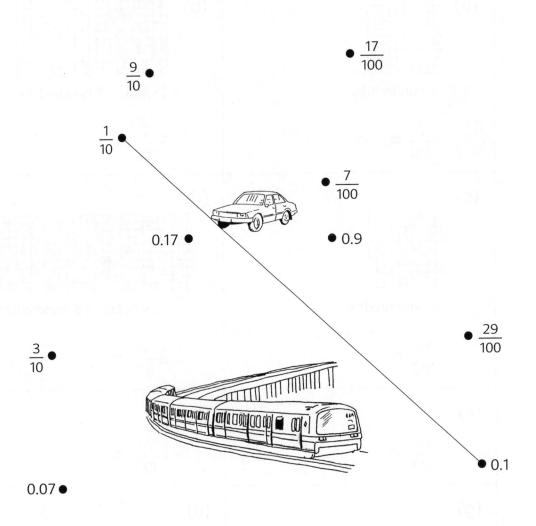

● $\frac{17}{100}$

$\frac{9}{10}$ ●

$\frac{1}{10}$ ●

● $\frac{7}{100}$

0.17 ●

● 0.9

● $\frac{29}{100}$

$\frac{3}{10}$ ●

● 0.1

0.07 ●

$\frac{7}{10}$ ●

● $\frac{9}{100}$

0.29 ●

● 0.3

0.09 ●

● 0.7

EXERCISE 7

1. Write the value of each of the following as a decimal.

    (a) $80 + \dfrac{7}{10} =$

    (b) $20 + 4 + \dfrac{5}{10} =$

    (c) $34 + \dfrac{4}{100} =$

    (d) $7 + \dfrac{2}{10} + \dfrac{9}{100} =$

2. Fill in the missing fractions.

    (a) $4.37 = 4 + \dfrac{3}{10} + $ _____

    (b) $3.05 = 3 + $ _____

    (c) $80.2 = 80 + $ _____

    (d) $1.76 = 1 + $ _____ $ + \dfrac{6}{100}$

    (e) $72.4 = 70 + 2 + $ _____

3. Fill in the missing decimals.

    (a) $8.24 = 8 + 0.2 + $ _____

    (b) $23.05 = 20 + 3 + $ _____

    (c) $7.14 = 7 + $ _____ $ + 0.04$

    (d) $5.08 = 5 + $ _____

    (e) $17.3 = 10 + 7 + $ _____

4. Complete the following number patterns.

   (a) 0.8, 0.9, _____, 1.1, _____, 1.3

   (b) 1, 1.5, 2, 2.5, _____, _____, 4

   (c) 3, 2.9, 2.8, _____, 2.6, _____, 2.4

   (d) 10, 9.5, 9, _____, 8, _____, 7

   (e) 0.05, 0.1, 0.15, _____, 0.25, _____, 0.35

   (f) 0.45, 0.4, 0.35, _____, _____, 0.2

   (g) 0.02, 0.04, 0.06, _____, 0.1, _____, 0.14

   (h) 10, 9.95, 9.9, _____, 9.8, _____, 9.7

5. Write the missing decimal in each box.

   (a)

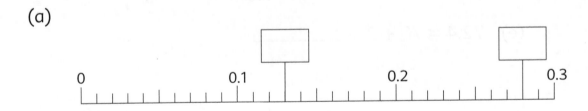

   (b)

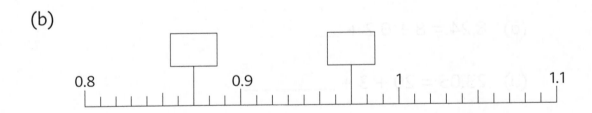

   (c)

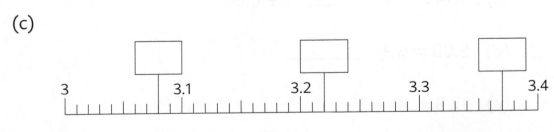

EXERCISE 8

1. Write each decimal as a fraction in its simplest form.

   (a) 0.5 =

   (b) 2.5 =

   (c) 0.08 =

   (d) 1.08 =

   (e) 0.15 =

   (f) 3.15 =

   (g) 0.64 =

   (h) 1.64 =

2. Change the denominator to 10.
   Then write the fraction as a decimal.

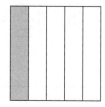 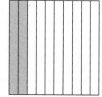

$$\frac{1}{5} = \frac{}{10} =$$

3. Change the denominator to 100.
   Then write the fraction as a decimal.

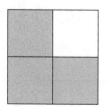 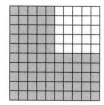

$$\frac{3}{4} = \frac{}{100} =$$

4. Change the denominator to 10 or 100.
   Then write the fraction as a decimal.

(a) $\dfrac{1}{2} = \dfrac{}{10}$	(b) $3\dfrac{1}{2} = 3\dfrac{}{10}$
$=$	$=$
(c) $\dfrac{3}{5} =$	(d) $1\dfrac{3}{5} =$
(e) $\dfrac{1}{4} =$	(f) $2\dfrac{1}{4} =$
(g) $\dfrac{4}{25} =$	(h) $1\dfrac{4}{25} =$

5. Write each fraction as a decimal.

(a) $\dfrac{4}{5} =$	(b) $3\dfrac{4}{5} =$
(c) $\dfrac{9}{20} =$	(d) $1\dfrac{9}{20} =$
(e) $\dfrac{3}{50} =$	(f) $2\dfrac{3}{50} =$

EXERCISE 9

1. Write **>** (is greater than), **<** (is less than) or **=** (is equal to) in each [   ].

(a)

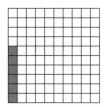

0.4 [   ] 0.06

(b)

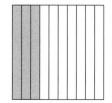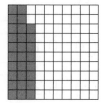

1.3 [   ] 1.28

(c)

4.23 [   ] 4.32

(d)

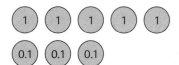

5.3 [   ] 3.54

25

2. Write > (is greater than), < (is less than) or = (is equal to) in each ▢.

(a) 2.01 ▢ 20.1

(b) 8.20 ▢ 0.82

(c) 7.23 ▢ 7.3

(d) 4.9 ▢ 0.59

(e) 1.50 ▢ 1.5

(f) 1.3 ▢ 0.13

(g) 0.10 ▢ 0.1

(h) 5.3 ▢ 3.55

3. Circle the smallest number in each set.

(a) 1.11,   1.2,   0.88,   2

(b) 6.1,   1.06,   6.01,   0.61

(c) 3.4,   2.99,   3.01,   4

(d) 4.2,   0.99,   2.4,   0.42

4. Circle the greatest number in each set.

(a) 2.89,   3,   2.9,   2.09

(b) 1.76,   1.8,   8.1,   1.08

(c) 5,   5.3,   5.03,   5.33

(d) 3.09,   7.01,   5.9,   4.6

EXERCISE 10

1. Fill in the blanks.

(a)

Hundreds	Tens	Ones	Tenths	Hundredths
(100) (100)	(10)	(1) (1)	(0.1) (0.1) (0.1)	(0.01) (0.01)
(100)	(10)	(1) (1)	(0.1) (0.1)	(0.01) (0.01)
				(0.01) (0.01)

(0.01)

_____ is 0.01 more than 324.56.

(b)

Hundreds	Tens	Ones	Tenths	Hundredths
(100)	(10) (10)	(1) (1)		(0.01) (0.01)
(100)	(10)	(1) (1)		(0.01) (0.01)
				(0.01)

(0.1)

_____ is 0.1 less than 234.15.

2. Fill in the blanks.

(a) _____ is 0.1 more than 46.05.

(b) _____ is 0.01 more than 39.2.

(c) _____ is 0.1 less than 60.08.

(d) _____ is 0.01 less than 42.5.

(e) 40 is _____ more than 39.9.

(f) 32.56 is _____ more than 32.55.

(g) 52.04 is _____ less than 52.14.

(h) 65 is _____ less than 65.01.

3. Add.

(a) 5.46 + 0.1 =	(b) 4.65 + 0.3 =
(c) 3.92 + 0.1 =	(d) 6.43 + 0.8 =
(e) 4.57 + 0.01 =	(f) 8.05 + 0.05 =
(g) 6.49 + 0.01 =	(h) 5.28 + 0.06 =

4. Subtract.

(a) 2.43 − 0.1 =	(b) 5.28 − 0.6 =
(c) 4.08 − 0.1 =	(d) 2.14 − 0.5 =
(e) 3.46 − 0.01 =	(f) 4.25 − 0.03 =
(g) 5.2 − 0.01 =	(h) 3.71 − 0.08 =

5. Write the missing number in each of the following:

(a)   (b)

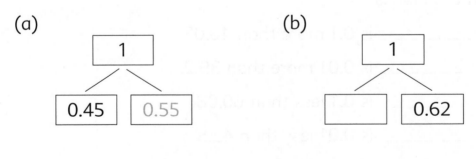

(c)   (d)

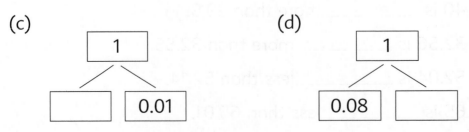

EXERCISE 11

1. Write a decimal for each of the following:

(a) $\boxed{0.001}$ $\boxed{0.001}$ $\boxed{0.001}$ $\boxed{0.001}$ 4 thousandths	
(b) $\boxed{1}$ $\boxed{1}$ $\boxed{0.001}$ $\boxed{0.001}$ $\boxed{0.001}$ $\boxed{0.001}$ $\boxed{0.001}$ $\boxed{1}$ $\boxed{1}$ $\boxed{0.001}$ $\boxed{0.001}$ 4 ones 7 thousandths	
(c) $\boxed{0.01}$ $\boxed{0.01}$ $\boxed{0.01}$ $\boxed{0.01}$ $\boxed{0.001}$ $\boxed{0.001}$ $\boxed{0.001}$ $\boxed{0.01}$ $\boxed{0.01}$ $\boxed{0.01}$ $\boxed{0.01}$ 8 hundredths 3 thousandths	
(d) $\boxed{0.1}$ $\boxed{0.1}$ $\boxed{0.01}$ $\boxed{0.01}$ $\boxed{0.001}$ $\boxed{0.001}$ $\boxed{0.001}$ $\boxed{0.1}$ $\boxed{0.1}$ $\boxed{0.01}$ $\boxed{0.001}$ $\boxed{0.001}$ 4 tenths 3 hundredths 5 thousandths	

2. Fill in the missing decimal in each of the following:

   (a) $6.723 = 6 + 0.7 + 0.02 + \boxed{}$

   (b) $35.406 = 35 + \boxed{}$

3. Fill in the missing fraction in each of the following:

   (a) $9.589 = 9 + \dfrac{5}{10} + \dfrac{8}{100} + \boxed{}$

   (b) $2.043 = 2 + \boxed{}$

29

4.

Ones	Tenths	Hundredths	Thousandths
3	4	7	9

Fill in the blanks.
(a) The number 3.479 is made up of _____ones, _____ tenths, _____ hundredths and _____ thousandths.

(b) In 3.479, the digit _____ is in the tenths place. The value of the digit is _____.

(c) The value of the digit 9 is _____.

(d) The value of the digit 7 is _____.

5. Write the missing decimal in each box.

(a)

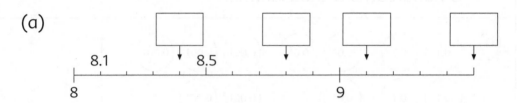

(b)

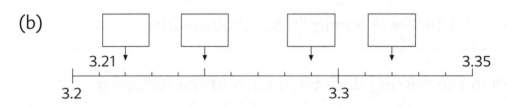

(c)

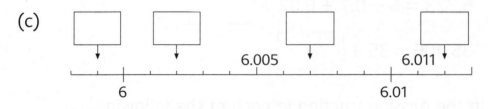

(d)

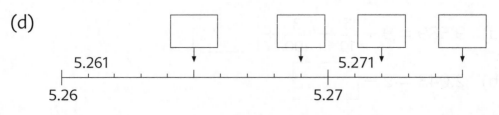

EXERCISE 12

1. Circle the greater number in each set.

   (a) 4.602,   4.7   (b) 9.1,   9.05

   (c) 1.924,   1.828   (d) 5,   0.52

2. Circle the greatest number in each set.

   (a) 24.68,   264.8,   64.82,   624.8

   (b) 5.073,   5.73,   5.307,   5.037

   (c) 0.042,   0.109,   1.1,   0.91

3. Write **>** (is greater than), **<** (is less than) or **=** (is equal to) in each ☐ .

   (a) 8.26 ☐ 8.206

   (b) 7.001 ☐ 7.1

   (c) 10.81 ☐ 10.810

   (d) 9.345 ☐ 9.306

   (e) 6.34 ☐ 6.304

   (f) 6.002 ☐ 6.200

4. Arrange the set of numbers in increasing order.

   | 2.8 | | 2.128 | | 2.18 | | 2.218 |

   _____

5. Arrange the set of numbers in decreasing order.

   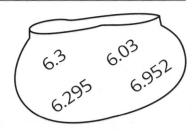

   6.3   6.03   6.295   6.952

   _____

31

EXERCISE 13

1. Express each decimal as a fraction in its simplest form.

(a) $0.64 = \dfrac{64}{100}$ $=$	(b) $0.38 =$
(c) $2.08 =$	(d) $4.95 =$
(e) $0.216 =$	(f) $0.352 =$
(g) $3.704 =$	(h) $2.425 =$

2. Circle the greatest number in each set.

(a) 2.5, $2\frac{1}{4}$, $2\frac{2}{5}$, 2.75

(b) 0.127, 0.2, $\frac{3}{25}$, 0.5

(c) 1.3, $\frac{3}{100}$, 0.9, $1\frac{1}{2}$

(d) $\frac{1}{2}$, 0.65, 0.45, $\frac{1}{5}$

3. Arrange the numbers in increasing order.

(a) 1.524, 1.245, 1.425, 1.254

_____

(b) 0.91, 0.19, 0.119, 0.097

_____

(c) $3\frac{1}{5}$, 3.95, $1\frac{9}{10}$, 2.5

_____

(d) $7\frac{1}{5}$, 7.5, $7\frac{3}{5}$, 7.1

_____

EXERCISE 14

1. Fill in the blanks.

(a)

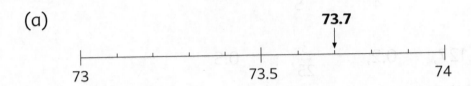

73.7 is _____ when rounded off to the nearest whole number.

(b)

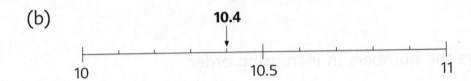

10.4 is _____ when rounded off to the nearest whole number.

(c)

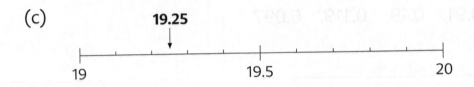

19.25 is _____ when rounded off to the nearest whole number.

(d)

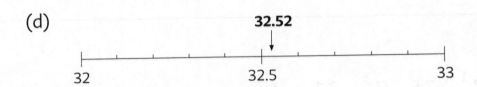

32.52 is _____ when rounded off to the nearest whole number.

2.

(a)	Ryan weighs 46.9 lb. Round off his weight to the nearest pound.	
(b)	A rope is 2.5 m long. Round off the length to the nearest meter.	
(c)	Sally drinks 1.25 ℓ of water a day. Round off the amount of water to the nearest liter.	
(d)	The distance between Town A and Town B is 29.38 km. Round off this distance to the nearest kilometer.	

3. Round off each of the following to the nearest dollar.

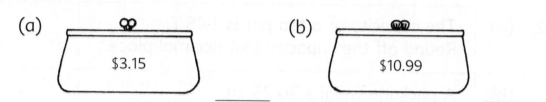

(a) $3.15

(b) $10.99

4. Round off each of the following to the nearest liter.

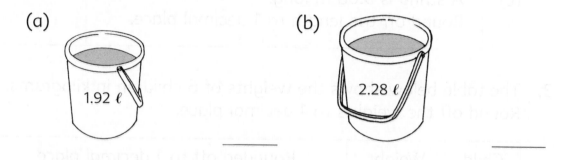

(a) 1.92 ℓ

(b) 2.28 ℓ

5. Round off each of the following to the nearest whole number.

(a) 39.8 _____

(b) 46.4 _____

(c) 6.39 _____

(d) 5.92 _____

(e) 101.5 _____

(f) 299.5 _____

EXERCISE 15

1. Fill in the blanks.

    (a)

    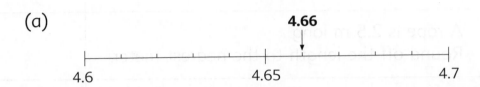

    4.66 is _____ when rounded off to 1 decimal place.

    (b)

    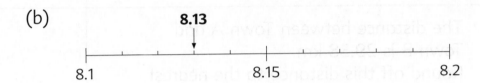

    8.13 is _____ when rounded off to 1 decimal place.

2.

(a)	The capacity of a tea pot is 1.45 ℓ. Round off the capacity to 1 decimal place.	
(b)	A package weighs 20.25 kg. Round off the weight to 1 decimal place.	
(c)	A string is 9.08 m long. Round off the length to 1 decimal place.	

3. The table below shows the weights of 6 children in kilograms.
    Round off the weights to 1 decimal place.

Child	Weight	Rounded off to 1 decimal place
A	34.91 kg	
B	41.68 kg	
C	39.75 kg	

REVIEW 1

Write the answers in the boxes.

1. Which one of the following numbers has the digit **4** in the hundreds place?

   92,**4**05,   24,905,   **4**9,250,   50,9**4**2

2. In 2**5**,364, the digit **5** is in the _____ place.

3. Write the next number in the following number pattern.

   26,495,   31,495,   36,495,   41,495

4. Write the missing number in each of the following:

   (a) 56,180 = 50,000 + _____ + 100 + 80

   (b) 40,000 + 2000 + 90 + 6 = _____

   (c) _____ is 1000 more than 89,800.

   (d) _____ is 1000 less than 28,481.

5. Which one of the following is the greatest?

   70,582,   78,502,   75,802,   78,205

6. Which one of the following is the smallest?

   3,   0.3,   0.03,   30

7. There were about 24,500 spectators at a football game. Which one of the following could be the actual number of spectators?

   24,561,   24,391,   24,519,   24,083

8. Write down the first two common multiples of 6 and 5.

9. Which one of the following is equal to $\frac{2}{3}$?

$\frac{8}{12}$, $\frac{6}{12}$, $\frac{3}{12}$, $\frac{2}{6}$

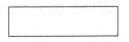

10. Which is greater, $\frac{3}{8}$ or $\frac{7}{12}$?

11. How many sixths are there in $2\frac{1}{6}$?

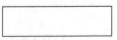

12. Express $3\frac{2}{5}$ as a decimal.

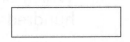

13. Write the decimal represented by each letter.

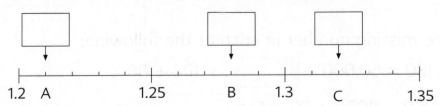

1.2   A   1.25   B   1.3   C   1.35

14. Complete the number pattern.

3.5,   4,   [   ] ,   [   ] ,   5.5

15. Arrange the following in order, beginning with the greatest.
2 m 35 cm,   253 cm,   2 km,   20 m

16. The table shows the savings of 4 boys.

Name	Savings
David	$44
Samy	$27
Ramat	$56
Sumin	$81

(a) How much more did Ramat save than David? [   ]

(b) Who saved 3 times as much as Samy? [   ]

17. Brandy bought 3 yd of raffia.

She used $\frac{5}{6}$ yd to make a doll.

Find the length of the raffia left.

18. After selling $\frac{1}{2}$ of his apples, Carlos had 15 apples left.

How many apples did he have at first?

19. John made 15 flower pot hangers.

He used $\frac{2}{3}$ m of wire for each hanger.

Find the length of wire he used altogether.

20. Measure the marked angle.

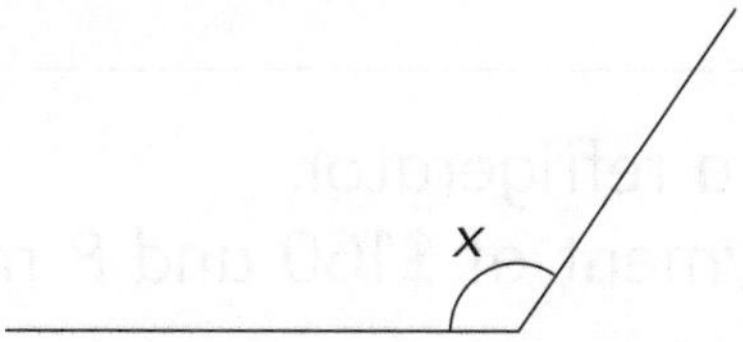

x

21. Which one of the marked angles in the figure is greater than 2 right angles?

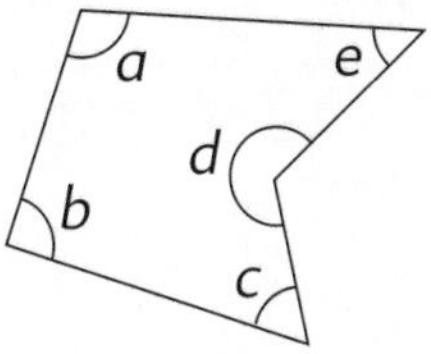

a e

d

b

c

22. Find $\angle y$ in the rectangle.

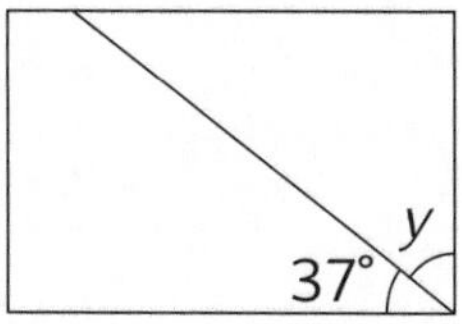

y

$37°$

23. Ben had $35.

He spent $\frac{2}{7}$ of it on a pair of shoes.

How much money did he have left?

24. 1650 students took part in a parade.
    There were twice as many boys as girls.
    How many boys were there in the parade?

25. Mrs. Rowley bought a refrigerator.
    She paid a down payment of $160 and 8 monthly installments
    of $95 each.
    How much did she pay altogether?

26. There are 36 students in a class.

$\frac{2}{3}$ of them are girls.

$\frac{1}{4}$ of the girls wear glasses.

How many girls wear glasses?

---

27. The rectangle has the same perimeter as the square.
Find the length of each side of the square.

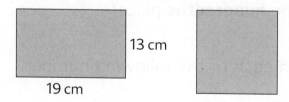

13 cm

19 cm

REVIEW 2

Write the answers in the boxes.

1. What is the greatest 5-digit number that can be formed using all of the digits 0, 1, 9, 5 and 8?

2. What does each of the digits in 96,383 stand for?

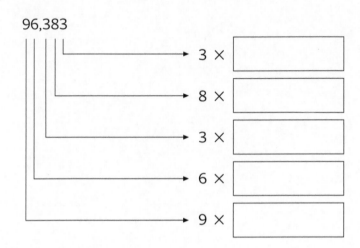

96,383

3 × ☐

8 × ☐

3 × ☐

6 × ☐

9 × ☐

3. The value of the digit **6** in 32.**6**4 is ☐ .

4. In 30.49, which digit is in the **hundredths** place? ☐

5. Write the missing number in each of the following number patterns.

   (a) 50,230, ☐ , 46,230, 44,230

   (b) 71.54, 71.04, ☐ , 70.04

6. How much is $\frac{2}{5}$ of $10? ☐

7. Express 1100 g as a fraction of 2 kg. ☐

8. Write each fraction as a decimal.

(a) $5\frac{1}{4}$

(b) $16\frac{4}{5}$

9. Write each decimal as a fraction in its simplest form.

(a) 0.85

(b) 2.4

10. In 23.56, which digit is in the **tenths** place?

11. Which one of the following is the greatest?

49.05, 495, 4.95, 45.09

12. Round off 6.29 to 1 decimal place.

13. Round off $35.05 to the nearest dollar.

14. What is the missing number in each ■?

(a) ■ is 0.01 more than 6.04.

(b) ■ is 0.1 less than 3.8.

(c) $5.61 = 5 +$ ■

(d) $16.7 = 10 +$ ■

15. Write > (is greater than), < (is less than) or = (is equal to) in each ☐.

(a) 12.62 ☐ 12.26

(b) 8.70 ☐ 8.7

16. David took 3 hours 25 minutes to paint his room.
He finished painting his room at 1:40 p.m.
At what time did he start painting his room?

17. The stadium is 4 km 360 m from Nicky's apartment.
It is 1 km 250 m from Brian's apartment.
How much further is the stadium from Nicky's apartment
than from Brian's apartment?

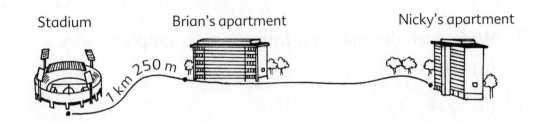

Stadium   Brian's apartment   Nicky's apartment

18. Taylor made 98 sugar cookies and 42 chocolate cookies.
What fraction of the cookies were chocolate cookies?

19. Roger spent $\frac{1}{5}$ of his monthly salary on food.

He spent twice as much money on transport as on food.
What fraction of his monthly salary was spent on transport?

20. The total weight of two bags of flour is 2 lb.

One of them weighs $\frac{1}{4}$ lb.

What is the weight of the other bag of flour?

21. Joe had $24.

He used $\frac{3}{8}$ of it to buy a book.

What was the cost of the book?

44

22. A rectangular garden measures 35 m by 24 m. What is the cost of putting up a fence around the garden if 1 m of fencing costs $10?

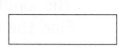

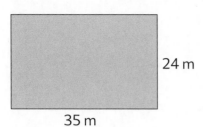

24 m

35 m

23. The area of a rectangular vegetable plot is 35 yd². If the length of the vegetable plot is 7 yd, find its width.

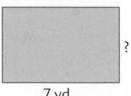

?

7 yd

24. In the figure, ∠XYZ is 46°. Measure ∠WYZ.

X

Y 46° ———— Z

?

W

25.

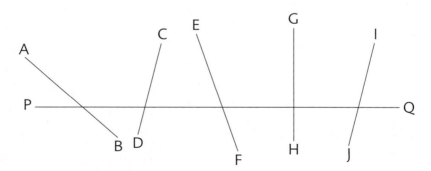

(a) Name a pair of parallel lines.

(b) Name a pair of perpendicular lines.

26. The perimeter of a rectangle is 48 in.
    The length of the rectangle is twice its width.
    Find the length of the rectangle.

27. There are 84 children in a choir.

    $\frac{5}{6}$ of them are girls.

    How many boys are there?

REVIEW 3

Write the answers in the boxes.

1. What number does each letter represent?

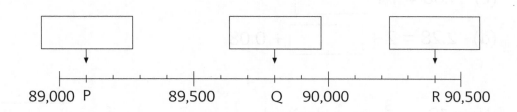

89,000 P   89,500   Q   90,000   R 90,500

2. Write the missing number in each of the following:

   (a) 36,495 = 30,000 + ☐ + 400 + 95

   (b) ☐ is 100 more than 49,912.

   (c) ☐ is 10,000 less than 63,045.

3. When 48,329 is written as 48,300, it is rounded off to the nearest ☐.

4. Round off $15,017 to the nearest $10. ☐

5. Mrs. Cohen bought a dress which cost about $23. Which one of the following could be the actual cost of the dress?

   $22.10, $23.95, $22.50, $23.50 ☐

6. In 8.**62**, the value of the digit **2** is ☐.

7. In 62.85, which digit is in the **hundredths** place? ☐

8. Write the missing number in each of the following:

(a) [ ] is 0.01 more than 20.99.

(b) [ ] is 0.01 less than 48.03.

(c) $1.06 = 1 +$ [ ]

(d) $2.28 = 2 +$ [ ] $+ 0.08$

9. Write $10 + \dfrac{3}{100}$ as a decimal. [ ]

10. Arrange the numbers in increasing order.
40.62, 40.26, 42.06, 42.6

[ ]

11. Find the product of 14 and 35. [ ]

12. What fraction of the figure is shaded? [ ]

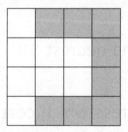

13. Write $\dfrac{24}{15}$ in its simplest form. [ ]

14. Ali spent $36 in a shop.

$\dfrac{1}{9}$ of the money was spent on a toy.

What was the cost of the toy? [ ]

48

15. A carton contains 250 ml of fruit juice.
    How much fruit juice can you get from 6 such cartons?
    Give your answer in liters and milliliters.

16. Write the missing number in each of the following:

    (a) 4 ℓ 650 ml = [   ] ml

    (b) 2 km 634 m = [   ] m

    (c) 5 kg 107 g = [   ] g

    (d) 3 h 4 min = [   ] min

    (e) 260 min = [   ] h [   ] min

    (f) 4007 g = [   ] kg [   ] g

    (g) 580 cm = [   ] m [   ] cm

    (h) 3020 ml = [   ] ℓ [   ] ml

    (i) 108 oz = [   ] lb [   ] oz

17. The area of a square is 64 in.²
    (a) Find the length of one side of the square.
    (b) Find the perimeter of the square.

18. Find the area of the figure. (All lines meet at right angles.)

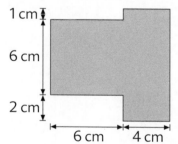

19. How many right angles are equal to $\frac{1}{2}$ of a complete turn?

20. Measure ∠x and ∠y.

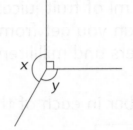

∠x =

∠y =

21. Mark a right angle (⌐) to show a pair of perpendicular lines.
    Draw arrowheads (//) to show a pair of parallel lines.

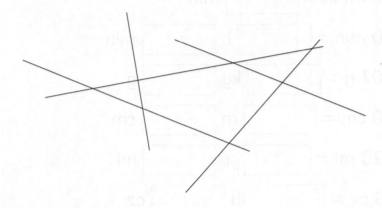

22. A pineapple weighs 1 kg 680 g.
    A papaya is 800 g lighter than the pineapple.
    Find the total weight of the two fruits.

23 ABCD is a rectangle and DCEF is a square.
    The perimeter of the square DCEF is 20 cm.
    The perimeter of the rectangle ABCD is 36 cm.
    Find the length of the rectangle ABCD.

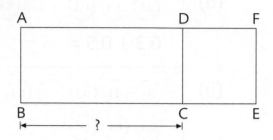

24. Alice bought a reel of thread 6 m long.

    She cut off 4 pieces of thread, each $\frac{1}{5}$ m long, from the reel.

    Find the length of the remaining thread.

EXERCISE 16

1. Add.

(a)

0.3 + 0.5 =

(b)

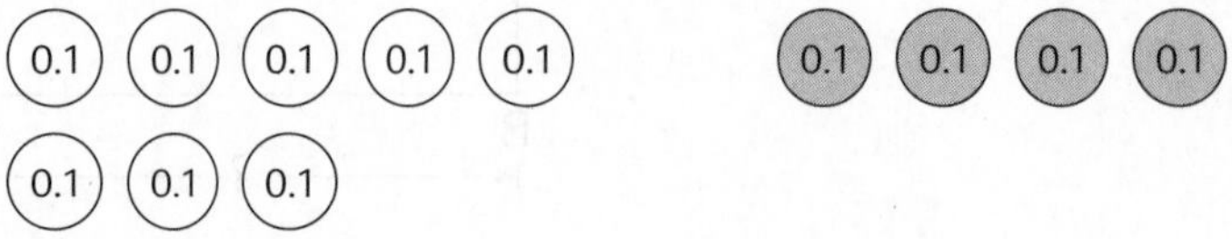

0.8 + 0.4 =

(c) | 0.2 + 0.4 =

(d) | 0.9 + 0.1 =

(e) | 0.5 + 0.9 =

2. Add.

(a)

0.04 + 0.02 =

(b)

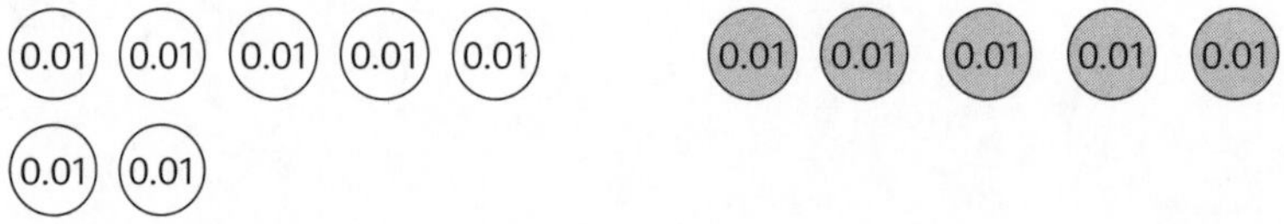

0.07 + 0.05 =

(c) | 0.03 + 0.02 =

(d) | 0.09 + 0.01 =

(e) | 0.07 + 0.04 =

EXERCISE 17

1. Add.

(a)

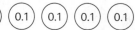

2.6 + 0.5 =

(b)

2.4 + 3 =

(c) 4.5 + 6 =

(d) 5.4 + 0.8 =

2. Add.

(a) 3.2 + 1.8 =	(b) 4.6 + 3.7 =
$\begin{array}{r} 3\,.\,2 \\ +\ 1\,.\,8 \\ \hline \end{array}$	
(c) 5.9 + 7.8 =	(d) 8.4 + 7.9 =

EXERCISE 18

1. Add.

(a)

2.53 + 0.2 =

(b)

2.53 + 0.02 =

(c) 4.65 + 0.4 =

(d) 3.87 + 0.7 =

(e) 5.34 + 0.9 =

(f) 3.82 + 0.06 =

(g) 2.63 + 0.07 =

(h) 4.29 + 0.05 =

2. Add.

(a) 0.65 + 0.27 = $$\begin{array}{r} 0.65 \\ +\ 0.27 \\ \hline \end{array}$$	(b) 0.64 + 2.39 =
(c) 1.8 + 0.56 =	(d) 24.48 + 3.8 =
(e) 1.43 + 2.19 =	(f) 8.25 + 1.36 =
(g) 12.84 + 4.5 =	(h) 46.75 + 21.43 =

55

EXERCISE 19

1. Add.

14.74 + 28.16 **D**	8.65 + 11.86 **S**	41.8 + 2.29 **Q**	66.19 + 23.81 **M**
5.06 + 6.3 **O**	27.8 + 39.1 **N**	21 + 12.6 **M**	54.45 + 8.55 **U**
24.81 + 2.54 **I**	31.4 + 57.35 **J**	60 + 8.05 **A**	77.99 + 4.01 **V**

Write the letters which match the answers.
You will find the name of Singapore's national flower.

82	68.05	66.9	42.9	68.05

33.6	27.35	20.51	20.51

88.75	11.36	68.05	44.09	63	27.35	90

EXERCISE 20

1. Subtract.

(a)
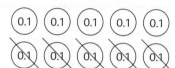

$1 - 0.4 =$

(b)
0.1 0.1 0.1 0.1 0.1   0.1 0.1 0.1 0.1

0.1 0.1 0.1 0.1 0.1

$1.4 - 0.5 =$

(c) $1.2 - 0.9 =$

(d) $4.3 - 0.4 =$

2. Subtract.

(a) $5.7 - 0.4 =$

$$\begin{array}{r} 5\,.\,7 \\ -\ 0\,.\,4 \\ \hline \end{array}$$

(b) $3.1 - 0.5 =$

(c) $4.06 - 0.9 =$

(d) $3 - 0.8 =$

EXERCISE 21

1. Subtract.

(a)

0.08 − 0.03 =

(b)

1 − 0.35 =

(c) 0.9 − 0.05 =

(d) 1 − 0.08 =

2. Subtract.

(a)

4.41 − 0.03 =

(b)

1.5 − 0.02 =

3. Subtract.

(a) 0.48 − 0.06 $$\begin{array}{r} 0.48 \\ -\ 0.06 \\ \hline \end{array}$$	(b) 3.27 − 0.03 =
(c) 2.83 − 0.05 =	(d) 6.15 − 0.09 =
(e) 2.7 − 0.08 =	(f) 4.3 − 0.07 =
(g) 5.1 − 0.06 =	(h) 4 − 0.09 =

EXERCISE 22

1. Subtract.

(a) $3.7 - 1.6 =$ $\begin{array}{r} 3\,.\,7 \\ -\ 1\,.\,6 \\ \hline \end{array}$	(b) $5.6 - 2.9 =$
(c) $7.4 - 3.8 =$	(d) $4.3 - 2.7 =$
(e) $4 - 1.8 =$	(f) $7 - 5.6 =$
(g) $8 - 3.9 =$	(h) $6 - 2.4 =$

EXERCISE 23

1. Subtract.

(a) $8.74 - 6.3 =$ $\begin{array}{r} 8.74 \\ -\ 6.3 \\ \hline \end{array}$	(b) $6.45 - 3.9 =$
(c) $0.6 - 0.53 =$	(d) $9.5 - 0.72 =$
(e) $4.86 - 1.62 =$	(f) $8.41 - 3.65 =$
(g) $7 - 0.85 =$	(h) $10 - 4.57 =$

EXERCISE 24

1. Subtract.

4.91 − 2.56	8 − 4.92	0.9 − 0.47	12.05 − 7.4
T	**E**	**H**	**U**
9.4 − 4.73	1.38 − 0.6	16.42 − 9.18	3 − 1.63
R	**P**	**C**	**S**
11.76 − 4.38	10.06 − 5.9	15 − 6.04	10.6 − 3.82
I	**G**	**O**	**N**

What birds cannot fly?

Write the letters which match the answers.
You will find two of them.

0.78	3.08	6.78	4.16	4.65	7.38	6.78

8.96	1.37	2.35	4.67	7.38	7.24	0.43

EXERCISE 25

1. Write the missing numbers.

   (a) $5.24 \xrightarrow{\ +2\ }$ [ ] $\xrightarrow{\ -0.01\ }$ [ ]

   $5.24 + 1.99 =$ [ ]

   (b) $7.63 \xrightarrow{\ +4\ }$ [ ] $\xrightarrow{\ -0.05\ }$ [ ]

   $7.63 + 3.95 =$ [ ]

   (c) $4.82 \xrightarrow{\ -3\ }$ [ ] $\xrightarrow{\ +0.01\ }$ [ ]

   $4.82 - 2.99 =$ [ ]

   (d) $6.05 \xrightarrow{\ -2\ }$ [ ] $\xrightarrow{\ +0.02\ }$ [ ]

   $6.05 - 1.98 =$ [ ]

2. Add.

(a) $6.81 + 2.98 =$
(b) $8.69 + 1.95 =$

3. Subtract.

(a) $8.25 - 3.99 =$
(b) $7.53 - 2.95 =$

EXERCISE 26

1. Mitchell had a piece of wire 5 yd long.
    After using a length of it, he had 2.35 yd of wire left.
    How much wire did he use?

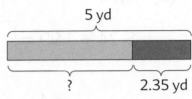

2. A baby boy weighed 3.6 kg at birth.
    After a month, he weighed 5 kg.
    How much weight did he gain?

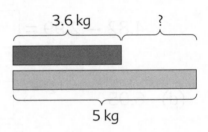

3. Mr. Smith brought $36.45 to a mall.
    He came home with $2.54.
    How much did he spend at the mall?

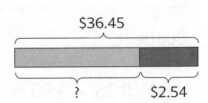

EXERCISE 27

1. Salmah had $13.50.
   She spent $1.40 on bus-fare and $2.50 on lunch.
   How much did she have left?

2. Betty bought a vase for $12 and a bunch of flowers for $4.50.
   She gave the salesgirl $20.
   How much change did she receive?

3. Mrs. Lee bought an iron and a kettle.
   The iron cost $38.90.
   The kettle cost $6.50 more than the iron.
   How much did she spend altogether?

---

4. Ribbon A is 0.38 ft longer than Ribbon B.
   Ribbon A is 0.25 ft shorter than Ribbon C.
   If Ribbon C is 1.63 ft long, find the length of Ribbon B.

EXERCISE 28

1. Multiply.

(a)

$0.4 \times 2 =$

(b)

$0.6 \times 3 =$

(c) $0.2 \times 7 =$

(d) $0.9 \times 4 =$

(e) $0.5 \times 6 =$

(f) $0.7 \times 8 =$

(g) $0.3 \times 9 =$

(h) $0.8 \times 5 =$

2. Multiply.

(a)

$0.03 \times 2 =$

(b)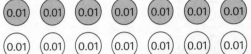

$0.07 \times 4 =$

(c) $0.02 \times 9 =$

(d) $0.05 \times 7 =$

(e) $0.06 \times 5 =$

(f) $0.09 \times 8 =$

(g) $0.04 \times 3 =$

(h) $0.08 \times 6 =$

EXERCISE 29

1. Multiply.

(a) $4.3 \times 2 =$ $\begin{array}{r} 4\,.\,3 \\ \times \quad 2 \\ \hline \end{array}$	(b) $6.4 \times 3 =$
(c) $2.8 \times 6 =$	(d) $4.7 \times 9 =$
(e) $6.9 \times 4 =$	(f) $7 \times 5.5 =$
(g) $26.5 \times 5 =$	(h) $8 \times 30.6 =$

EXERCISE 30

1. Multiply.

(a) $0.83 \times 2 =$ $\begin{array}{r} 0\,.\,8\;3 \\ \times \qquad 2 \\ \hline \end{array}$	(b) $0.12 \times 6 =$
(c) $5.26 \times 3 =$	(d) $6.75 \times 4 =$
(e) $7.03 \times 6 =$	(f) $8 \times 5.64 =$
(g) $82.78 \times 7 =$	(h) $9 \times 64.72 =$

EXERCISE 31

1. Multiply.

0.48 × 2	20.3 × 4	0.03 × 7	4.91 × 3
L	**H**	**E**	**Y**
6.45 × 5	93.5 × 6	80.7 × 9	7.16 × 9
T	**E**	**P**	**E**
12.15 × 3	408.2 × 8	14.47 × 2	13.08 × 6
N	**D**	**H**	**E**

Write the letters which match the answers.
You will find a message.

81.2	561	0.96	726.3

32.25	28.94	0.21

36.45	64.44	78.48	3265.6	14.73

71

EXERCISE 32

1. Lynn bought 3 pieces of ribbon each 1.25 yd long.
   Find the total length of the ribbon.

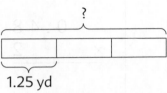

2. A bucket can hold 5.7 liters of water.
   A fish tank can hold 5 times as much water as the bucket.
   Find the capacity of the fish tank.

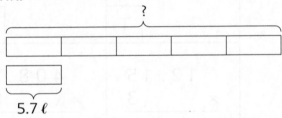

3. Cameron saved $2.50 a week for 6 weeks.
   How much did he save altogether?

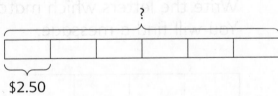

EXERCISE 33

1.   Complete the following bills.

Chocolates **Crackers** 1 can for $6.90 1 package for $1.45	1 can of chocolates $ _____ 2 packages of crackers $ _____ Total $ _____
Nuts **Sauce** 1 bag for $3.75 1 bottle for 95¢	2 bags of nuts $ _____ 2 bottles of sauce $ _____ Total $ _____
Bath towels **Face towels** $9.95 each $1.20 each	1 bath towel $ _____ 4 face towels $ _____ Total $ _____
Teddy bear **Dolls** $16.50 $8 each	3 dolls $ _____ 1 teddy bear $ _____ Total $ _____

73

2. Siti bought a piece of material 5 m long.
   She made 2 pillow cases.
   If she used 0.85 m of material for each pillow case, how much
   material did she have left?

---

3. Mimi spent $1.35 a day for 6 days.
   She had $2.50 left.
   How much money did she have at first?

EXERCISE 34

1. Divide.

(a)

0.8 ÷ 2 =

(b)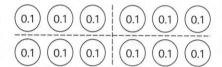

1.2 ÷ 4 =

(c) 0.9 ÷ 3 =

(d) 2.4 ÷ 6 =

(e) 2.8 ÷ 7 =

(f) 3 ÷ 5 =

(g) $6.30 ÷ 9 =

(h) $4.20 ÷ 7 =

2. Divide.

(a)

$$(0.01) \ (0.01) \ (0.01) \ | \ (0.01) \ (0.01) \ (0.01)$$

$$(0.01) \ (0.01) \ (0.01) \ | \ (0.01) \ (0.01) \ (0.01)$$

$0.12 \div 2 =$

(b)

$$(0.01) \ (0.01) \ (0.01) \ (0.01) \ (0.01)$$

$$(0.01) \ (0.01) \ (0.01) \ (0.01) \ (0.01)$$

$$(0.01) \ (0.01) \ (0.01) \ (0.01) \ (0.01)$$

$0.15 \div 3 =$

(c) $0.08 \div 2 =$

(d) $0.24 \div 4 =$

(e) $0.3 \div 5 =$

(f) $0.42 \div 7 =$

(g) $\$0.54 \div 6 =$

(h) $\$0.40 \div 8 =$

76

EXERCISE 35

1. Divide.

(a) $0.48 \div 2 =$ $2\overline{)0.48}$	(b) $0.63 \div 3 =$
(c) $0.65 \div 5 =$	(d) $0.95 \div 5 =$
(e) $0.84 \div 3 =$	(f) $0.68 \div 4 =$
(g) $0.78 \div 6 =$	(h) $0.96 \div 8 =$

2. Find the unit cost of each item below.

(a) 8 towels cost $7.60.

1 towel costs _____

(b) 4 notebooks cost $3.40.

1 notebook costs _____

(c) 3 erasers cost $1.05.

1 eraser costs _____

(d) 2 pears cost $1.80.

1 pear costs _____

EXERCISE 36

1. Divide.

(a) 8.26 ÷ 2 = $2\overline{)8.26}$	(b) 9.66 ÷ 3 =
(c) 7.35 ÷ 5 =	(d) 5.36 ÷ 2 =
(e) 68.25 ÷ 3 =	(f) 42.16 ÷ 8 =
(g) 80.56 ÷ 4 =	(h) 35.25 ÷ 5 =

2. Divide.

(a) $4\overline{)\$4.20}$	(b) $8\overline{)\$9.20}$
(c) $5\overline{)\$7.25}$	(d) $7\overline{)\$9.45}$
(e) $6\overline{)\$6.90}$	(f) $5\overline{)\$5.45}$
(g) $3\overline{)\$7.65}$	(h) $9\overline{)\$15.75}$

EXERCISE 37

1. Divide.

(a) $7 \div 5 =$ $5 \overline{)7}$	(b) $6 \div 8 =$
(c) $0.5 \div 2 =$	(d) $3.8 \div 4 =$
(e) $6.2 \div 5 =$	(f) $7.5 \div 6 =$
(g) $33 \div 4 =$	(h) $46.8 \div 8 =$

2. Divide.

(a) $2\overline{)9.7}$	(b) $4\overline{)60.6}$
(c) $8\overline{)94}$	(d) $5\overline{)48.6}$
(e) $4\overline{)150}$	(f) $8\overline{)26}$
(g) $8\overline{)2}$	(h) $6\overline{)176.1}$

EXERCISE 38

1. Divide. Give each answer correct to 1 decimal place.

7)32.4	3)61	3)22.74	5)30.2
6)32.94	9)28.9	4)37	8)17.28

Color the spaces which
contain the answers.
What number does it show?

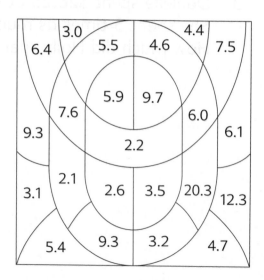

The number is _____.

EXERCISE 39

1. Jane cuts a rope 1.48 m long into 4 equal pieces.
   Find the length of each piece.

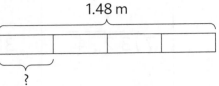

2. Mrs. Gray paid $20.40 for 3 kg of shrimps.
   Find the cost of 1 kg of shrimps.

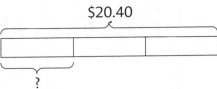

3. Danielle spent $28.25 at a bookshop.
   She spent 5 times as much as Holly.
   How much did Holly spend?

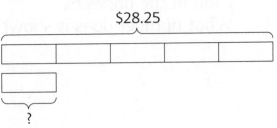

EXERCISE 40

1. Gwen and Susan bought the box of cookies and the tub of ice cream.
   They shared the cost equally.
   How much did each girl pay?

Cookies $3.15

Ice cream $4.65

2. Angela bought 5 kg of grapes.
   She gave the cashier $50 and received $18.75 change.
   Find the cost of 1 kg of grapes.

3. The total weight of 5 pieces of butter and a bag of flour is 2.7 lb.
   If the weight of the bag of flour is 1.2 lb, find the weight of each piece of butter.

---

4. A painter mixed 10.5 liters of white paint with 15.5 liters of red paint.
   He poured the mixture equally into 4 cans.
   How much paint was there in each can?

EXERCISE 41

1. Multiply and divide in compound units.

   (a) 2 ℓ 450 ml × 2 = _____ ℓ _____ ml

   (b) 2 m 65 cm × 3 = _____ m _____ cm

   (c) 6 km 250 m × 5 = _____ km _____ m

   (d) 3 kg 300 g ÷ 3 = _____ kg _____ g

   (e) 5 h 30 min ÷ 3 = _____ h _____ min

   (f) 1 ℓ 600 ml ÷ 4 = _____ ml

   (g) 4 lb 3 oz × 6 = _____ lb _____ oz

   (h) 2 ft 10 in. × 4 = _____ ft _____ in.

2. A bottle holds 1 ℓ 500 ml of water.
   A bucket holds 3 times as much water as the bottle.
   How much water can the bucket hold?

3. A fruit seller packed all his oranges into 6 boxes.
    Each box of oranges weighed 5 kg 500 g.
    What was the total weight of the oranges?

4. A washing machine takes 1 hour 40 minutes to wash one load
    of clothing.
    How long does it take to wash 4 loads of clothing?

5. Meredith had 6 kg 750 g of mushrooms.
    She packed them equally into 9 packets.
    What was the weight of each packet of mushrooms?

6. Johnny had 4 m 50 cm of wire.
   He cut the wire equally into 3 pieces.
   He used 2 pieces of the wire to repair his toy.
   (a) How long was each piece of wire?
   (b) What length of wire did he use to repair his toy?

---

7. A box containing 5 identical books weighs 6 kg 850 g.
   If the weight of the box is 600 g, what is the weight of each book?

REVIEW 4

Write the answers in the boxes.

1. Arrange the numbers in decreasing order.

    (a) 10,050, 9950, 9590, 10,590, 9190

    (b) 8.3, 2.83, 2.05, 7.28

2. Find the value of each of the following:

    (a) 54.86 + 2.9

    (b) 10.5 − 6.07

    (c) 60.45 ÷ 3

    (d) 35.25 × 8

3. (a) Round off the sum of 38.59 and 12.62 to 1 decimal place.

    (b) Round off the product of 4.85 and 9 to the
         nearest whole number.

4. What number is 0.7 more than 25.38?

5. Write the decimal represented by each letter.

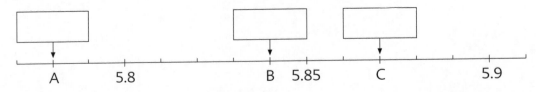

A   5.8   B   5.85   C   5.9

6. Jim left his home at 8:15 a.m.
   He returned at 5:50 p.m.
   How long was he away from home?

7. John is 1.7 m tall.
   His brother is 0.46 m shorter than he.
   How tall is his brother?

8. Miss Rowley made 4 jars of chocolate cookies and 6 jars of sugar cookies.
   There were 48 cookies in each jar.
   How many cookies did she make altogether?

9. Violet cut a cake into 8 equal pieces.
   She gave 2 pieces of the cake to her neighbor.
   What fraction of the cake did she have left?
   (Give the answer in its simplest form.)

10. Chris sleeps 8 hours a day.
    What fraction of a day does he sleep?

11. The capacity of a container is 4 gal.

    It contains $\frac{3}{5}$ gal of water.

    How much more water is needed to fill the container?

12. In a class of 40 students, $\frac{5}{8}$ of them can swim.

    How many students in the class **cannot** swim?

13. (a) In the figure, ABCD is a rectangle and ∠DAC = 57°.
    Measure ∠CAB.

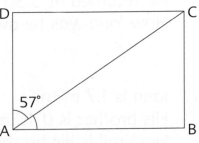

(b) In the figure, PQR is a straight line and ∠SQR = 136°.
    Measure ∠PQS.

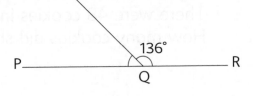

14. A can of beans costs $1.20.
    A can of peaches costs twice as much.
    What is the total cost of 1 can of beans and 2 cans of peaches?

15. Alice bought 6 ft of lace.
    She used 1 ft 3 in. of lace for a dress.
    She used 1 ft 8 in. of lace for another dress.
    How much lace did she have left?

---

16. Jamie bought 6 identical dictionaries as gifts for a party.
    The total weight of the dictionaries was 7 lb 8 oz.
    What was the weight of each dictionary?

REVIEW 5

Write the answers in the boxes.

1. What is the value of the digit **8** in **8**4,073?

2. Which one of the following is a **common factor** of 18 and 24?

    4, 6, 8, 12

3. Write the missing number in each of the following:

    (a) 86,049 is [   ] more than 76,049.

    (b) 39,561 is [   ] less than 40,561.

    (c) $7 \times 8 = 8 + 8 + $ [   ] $\times 8$

4. Arrange the numbers in increasing order.

    (a) 4.54, 25.4, 20.5, 5.04

    (b) 10.513, 5.013, 13.015, 3.515

5. Which one of the following has the digit **6** in the tenths place?

    1**6**.25, 12.**6**5, 15.2**6**, **6**2.15

6. The distance by air between City A and City B is 1444 km.
    Round off this distance to the nearest 100 km.

7. Write the missing number in each of the following:

(a) $38.56 = 30 + 8 + \boxed{} + 0.06$

(b) $93.72 = 90 + \boxed{}$

(c) $81.53 = 80 + 1 + \boxed{} + 0.03$

8. $3\dfrac{1}{4}$ is the same as $\dfrac{\boxed{}}{4}$.

9. Write the fraction represented by each letter.

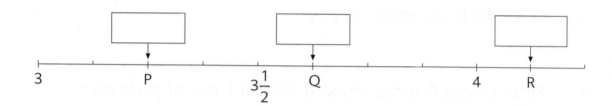

10. Which one of the following fractions is smaller than $\dfrac{1}{2}$?

$\dfrac{7}{8}$, $\dfrac{5}{9}$, $\dfrac{2}{5}$, $\dfrac{6}{11}$ $\boxed{}$

11. Arrange the fractions in order, beginning with the greatest.

$1\dfrac{1}{8}$, $\dfrac{3}{4}$, $1\dfrac{4}{5}$, $\dfrac{5}{6}$

$\boxed{}$

12. What fraction of 1 meter is 20 cm?
Write the fraction in its simplest form. $\boxed{}$

13. Jared has 98 stamps.
Tyrone has 153 more stamps than Jared.
How many stamps do they have altogether?

14. There are 14 boxes of cookies.
    There are 24 cookies in each box.
    How many cookies are there altogether?

15. There are 12 blocks of apartments in a housing project.
    There are 25 floors in each block of apartments.
    There are 4 apartments on each floor.
    How many apartments are there altogether?

16. Jack, John and Jim shared the cost of their lunch equally.
    The lunch cost $49.50.
    How much did each boy pay?

17. Peter jogged 6 times round a circular track of perimeter
    0.58 km.
    How many kilometers did he jog altogether?

18. There are 60 workers in a factory.
    48 of them are men.
    What fraction of the workers are women?

19. A tank is $\frac{5}{8}$ full.
    It contains 10 qt of water.
    What is the capacity of the tank?

20. David took 1 hour 35 minutes to travel from his house to
    the zoo.
    He left his house at 9:15 a.m.
    When did he arrive at the zoo?

21. How many hours and minutes are there from 10:45 p.m. to 1:30 a.m.?

22. Tom bought 10 twenty-cent stamps, 6 thirty-five-cent stamps and 8 fifty-cent stamps.
    How much did he spend altogether?

23. The table shows Larry's savings for 6 months. Find his total savings for the 6 months.

Month	Savings
January	$47
February	$58
March	$50
April	$64
May	$39
June	$36

24. The graph below shows the number of 4th grade students coming to school by school bus.

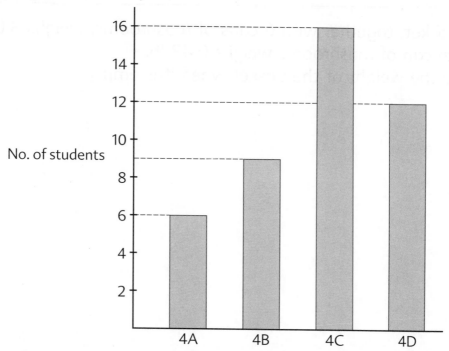

(a) Find the total number of students coming to school by school bus.
(b) Which class has the most number of students coming to school by school bus?

25. A computer costs $2290.

An oven costs $\frac{1}{5}$ the cost of the computer.

How much more does the computer cost than the oven?

---

26. A basket, together with 6 cans of mushrooms, weighs 3.05 lb.
Each can of mushrooms weighs 0.43 lb.
Find the weight of the basket when it is empty.

EXERCISE 42

1. Fold a piece of paper.
   Cut out a figure and then unfold it.
   You will get a symmetric figure.

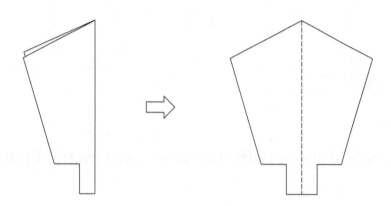

Complete the following symmetric figures.

(a)

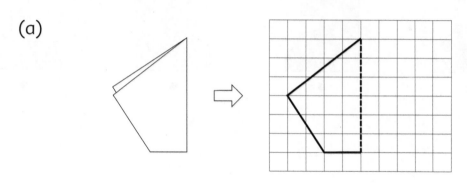

(b)

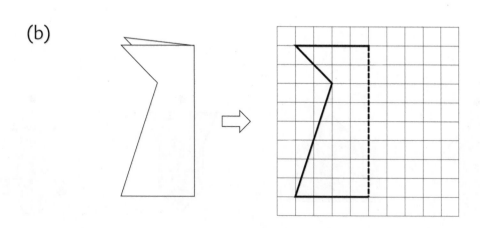

2. A symmetric figure can be cut out from a piece of paper like this:

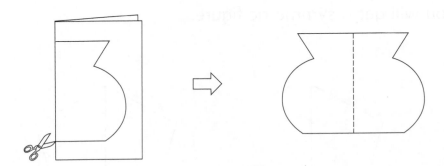

Match each of these with the correct symmetric figures below.

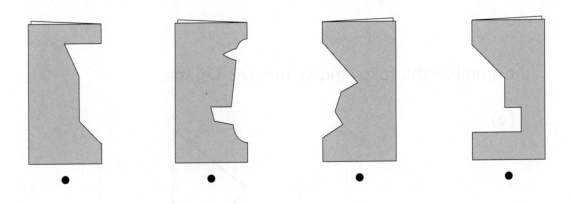

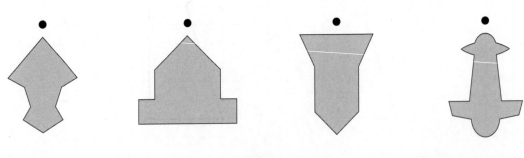

EXERCISE 43

1. Some of the following figures are symmetric figures.
   Draw a line of symmetry in each symmetric figure.

   (a)

   (b)

   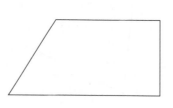

   (c)

   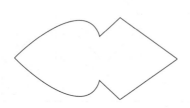

   (d)

   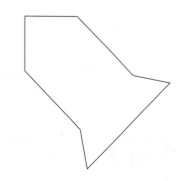

   (e)

   (f)

   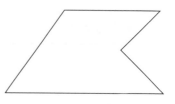

   (g)

   (h)

   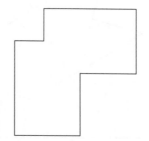

2. In each of the following figures, is the dotted line a line of symmetry? Write **Yes** or **No**.

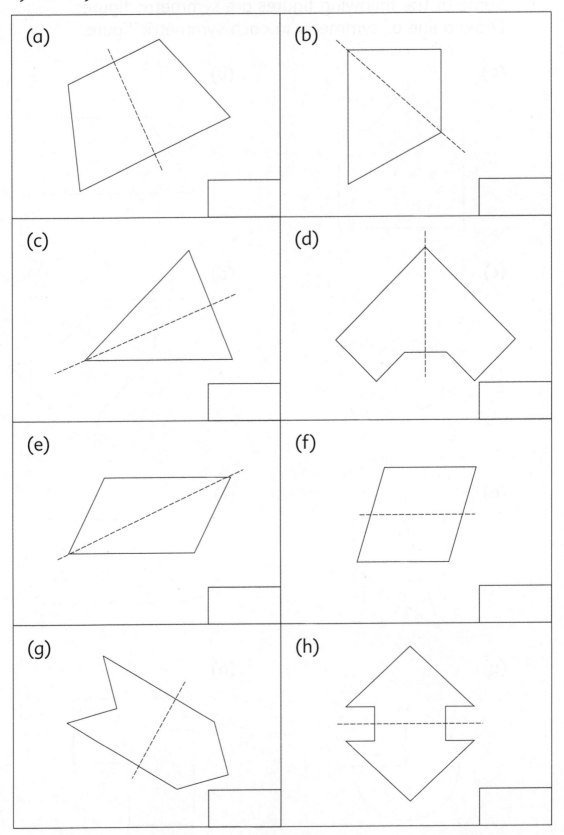

(a)

(b)

(c)

(d)

(e)

(f)

(g)

(h)

EXERCISE 44

1. Each of the following shows half of a letter.
    Draw the other half of each letter.
    (The dotted line is a line of symmetry.)

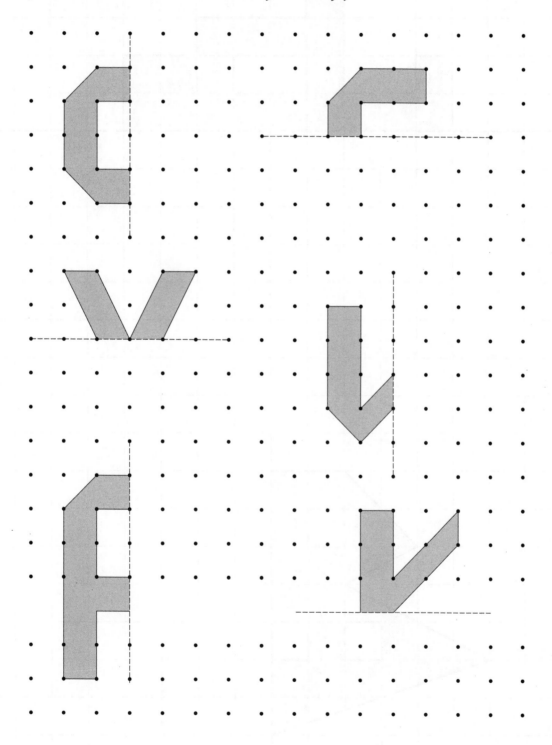

2. Use the dotted line as a line of symmetry.
   Complete the following symmetric figures.

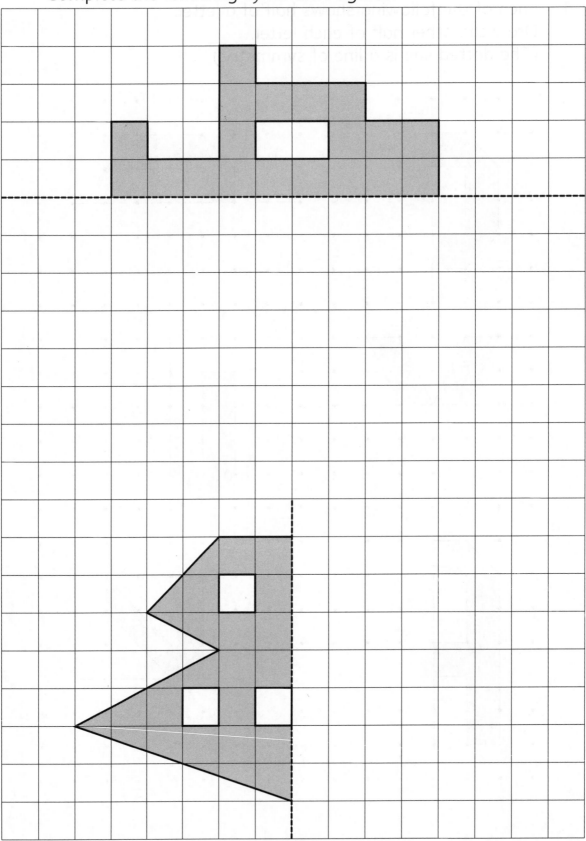

EXERCISE 45

1. Use unit cubes to build each solid.
   How many unit cubes are needed to build each solid?

(a)

(b)

(c)

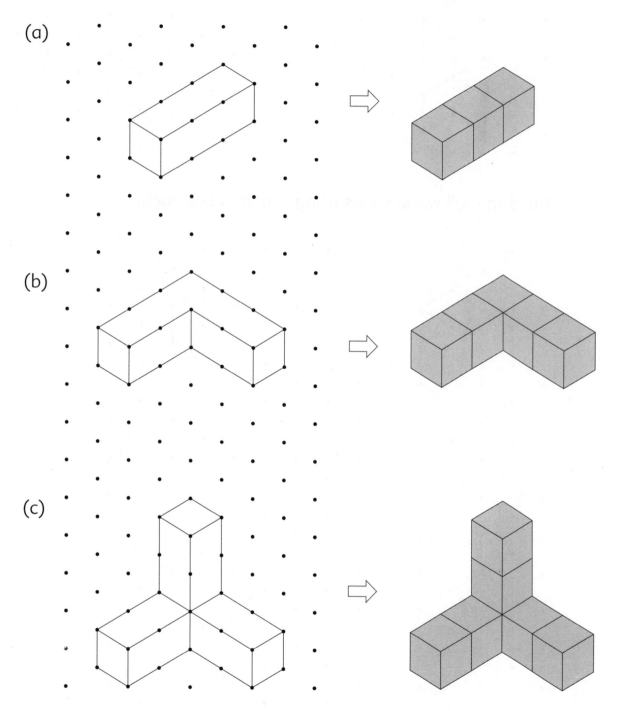

2. These two solids are built with 4 unit cubes each.

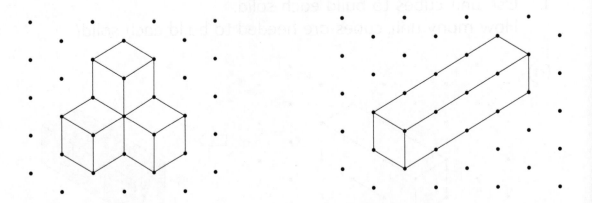

Build the following solids using 4 unit cubes each.

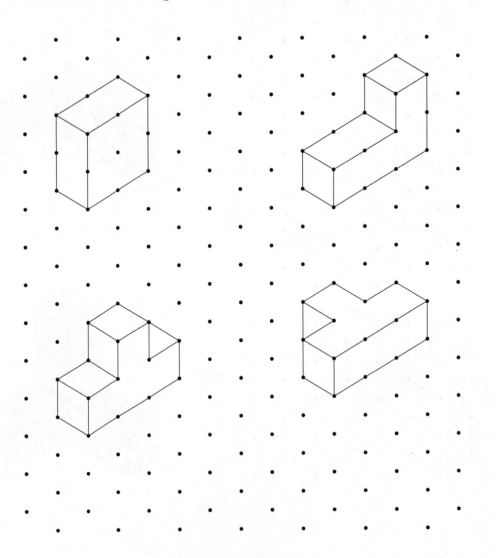

EXERCISE 46

1. Use unit cubes to build these solids.

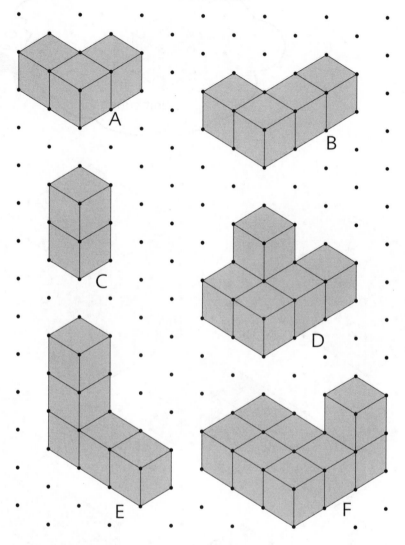

Then complete the following table.

Solid	Number of unit cubes
A	
B	
C	
D	
E	
F	

2. How many unit cubes are needed to build each of the following solids?

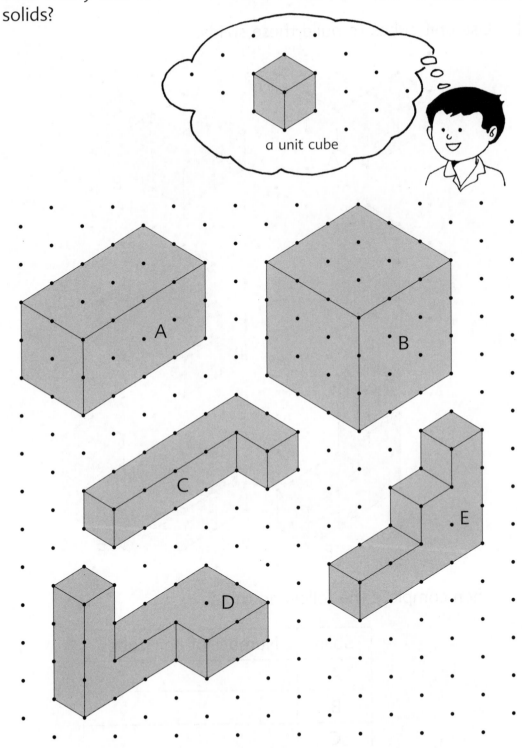

a unit cube

Solid	A	B	C	D	E
Number of unit cubes					

EXERCISE 47

1. Use unit cubes to build the solid on the left.
   Then remove some unit cubes to get the solid on the right.
   How many unit cubes are removed in each case?

(a)

(b)

(c)

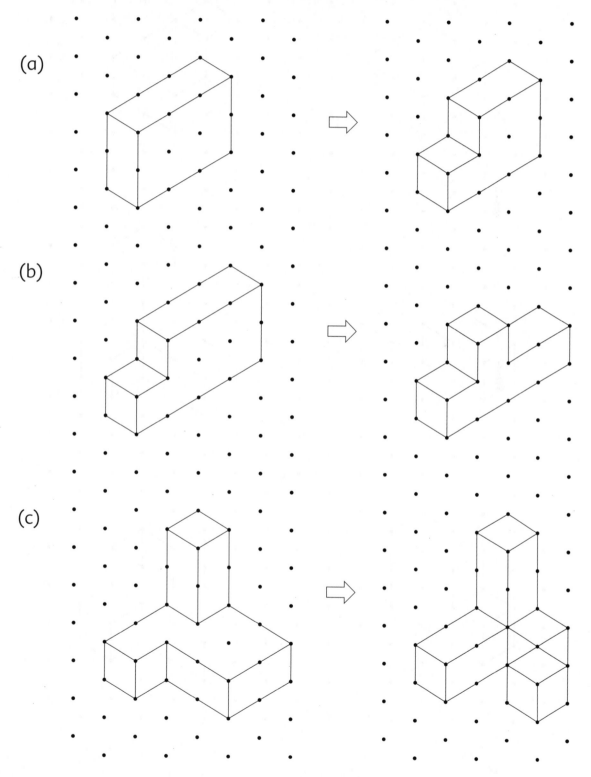

2. Use unit cubes to build the solid on the left. Then add some unit cubes to get the solid on the right.
   How many unit cubes are added in each case?

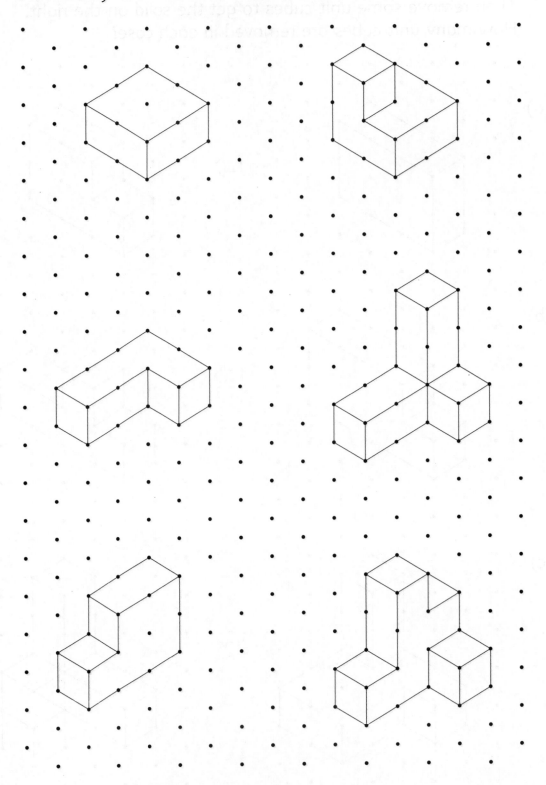

EXERCISE 48

1. What is the volume of each solid?

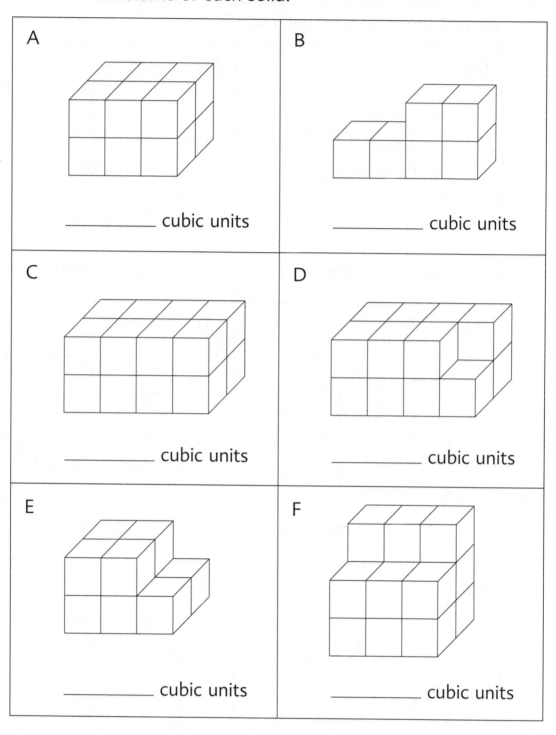

A

_____ cubic units

B

_____ cubic units

C

_____ cubic units

D

_____ cubic units

E

_____ cubic units

F

_____ cubic units

Which solid has the greatest volume? _____

Which solid has the smallest volume? _____

EXERCISE 49

1. The following solids are made up of 1-cm cubes.
    What is the volume of each solid?

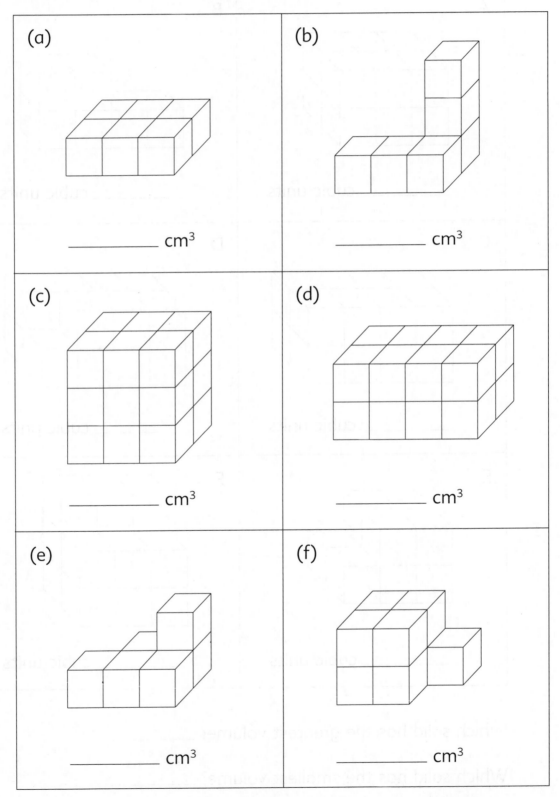

(a) _____ cm³

(b) _____ cm³

(c) _____ cm³

(d) _____ cm³

(e) _____ cm³

(f) _____ cm³

EXERCISE 50

1. These solids are made up of 1-in. cubes.

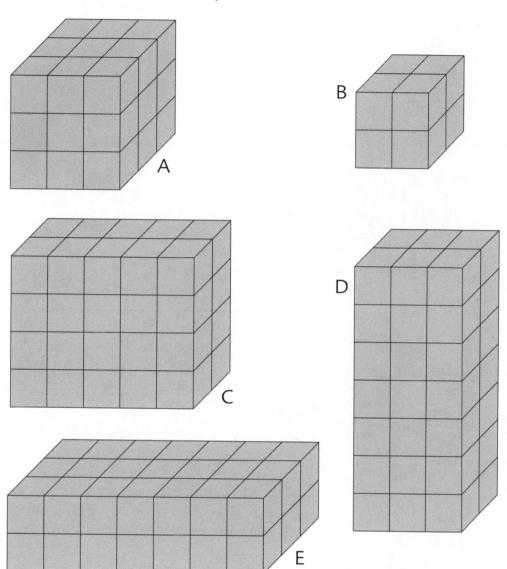

Complete the following table.

Solid	Length	Width	Height	Volume
A	3 in.	3 in.	3 in.	27 in.³
B				
C				
D				
E				

2. Find the volume of each cuboid.

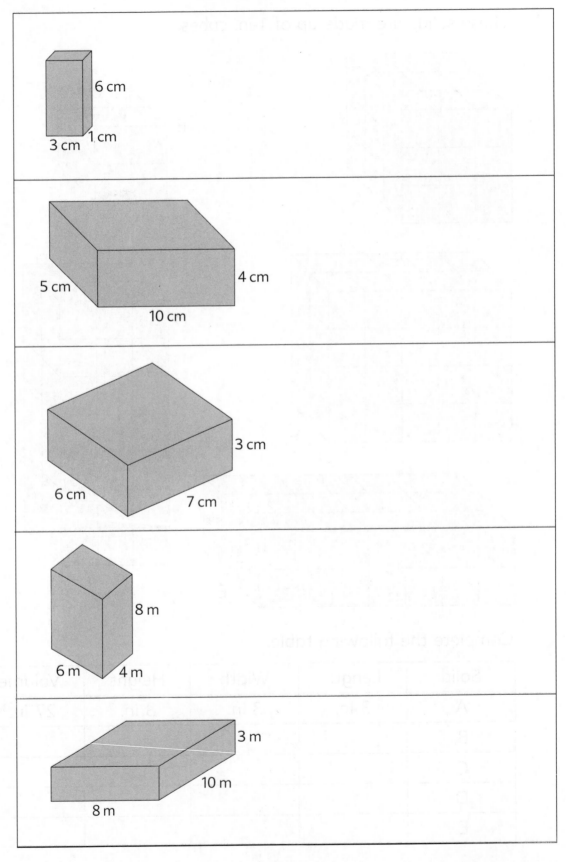

EXERCISE 51

1. Write the volume of the water in cubic centimeters.
   (1 ℓ = 1000 cm³)

   (a)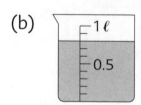

   _____ cm³

   (b)

   _____ cm³

2. Write the volume of the water in milliliters. (1 ml = 1 cm³)

   (a)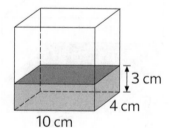

   _____ ml

   (b)

   _____ ml

3. Write the volume of the water in liters. (1 ℓ = 1000 cm³)

   (a)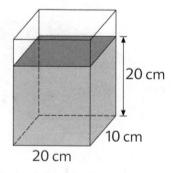

   _____ ℓ

   (b)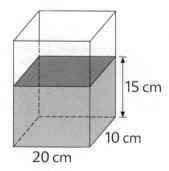

   _____ ℓ

4. Find the volume of the water in liters and milliliters.

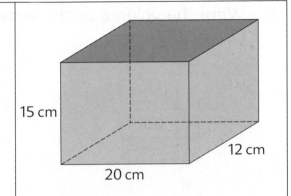

15 cm

8 cm

10 cm

The volume of the water

is _____.

15 cm

20 cm

12 cm

The volume of the water

is _____.

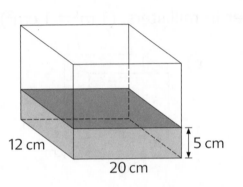

12 cm

20 cm

5 cm

The volume of the water

is _____.

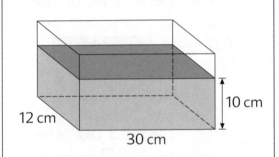

12 cm

30 cm

10 cm

The volume of the water

is _____.

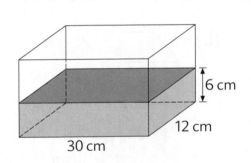

6 cm

12 cm

30 cm

The volume of the water

is _____.

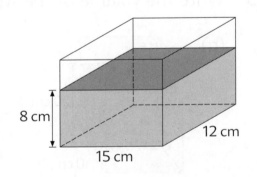

8 cm

15 cm

12 cm

The volume of the water

is _____.

REVIEW 6

Write the answers in the boxes.

1. Write the missing number in each of the following:

    (a) [   ] is 1000 more than 78,031.

    (b) [   ] is 1000 less than 56,100.

    (c) [   ] is 0.01 more than 23.28.

    (d) [   ] is 0.01 less than 18.22.

2. (a) In 32,105, which digit is in the **hundreds** place?

   (b) In 0.891, which digit is in the **hundredths** place?

   [   ]

   [   ]

3. (a) Round off $35,465 to the nearest $100.

   (b) Round off 8.09 m to the nearest meter.

   (c) Round off 16.72 yd to the nearest yard.

   [   ]

   [   ]

   [   ]

4. Complete the following number patterns.

   (a) $\frac{1}{6}$, $\frac{1}{3}$, $\frac{1}{2}$, [   ], $\frac{5}{6}$, [   ]

   (b) 2.75, 2.95, [   ], [   ], 3.55

5. Express $3\frac{5}{100}$ as a decimal.

   [   ]

6. Which one of the following is equal to $\frac{2}{5}$?

   0.2, 0.4, 2.5, 0.25

   [   ]

117

7. Which one of the following is a fraction in its simplest form?

   $\dfrac{3}{9}$, $\dfrac{2}{10}$, $\dfrac{5}{7}$, $\dfrac{4}{8}$

8. Express 2.4 as a fraction in its simplest form.

9. Find the value of each of the following:

   (a) 6 + 0.6 + 0.06

   (b) 0.3 – 0.03

   (c) 4.8 × 5

   (d) 2.2 ÷ 4

10. How many thirds are there in 3?

11. Divide 17 by 4.
    Give the answer correct to 1 decimal place.

12. A watermelon weighs 2 kg 450 g.
    A pineapple weighs 865 g.
    How much heavier is the watermelon than the pineapple?

13. A television set cost $1800.
    It cost 4 times as much as a digital camera.
    Find the total cost of the television set and the digital camera.

14. After buying 2 shirts at $12.50 each, David had $39.85 left.
    How much money did he have at first?

15. In a test, Muthu answered 32 out of 40 items correctly.
    What fraction of the items did he answer correctly?

    [ ]

16. David had $20.

    He spent $\frac{1}{10}$ of the money on lunch.
    How much did the lunch cost?

    [ ]

17. Draw a line parallel to PQ.

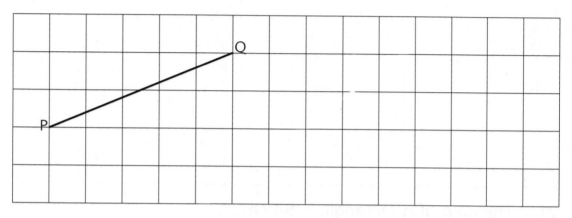

18. Draw an angle equal to 125°.

19. These solids are made up of 1-cm cubes.
    Find the difference in volume between them.

    [ ]

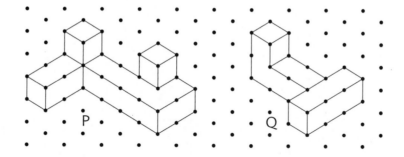

20. Reis received twice as much money as Ben.
    Ben received $14.80 less than Sam.
    If Sam received $61.20, how much money did Reis receive?

---

21. The area of a rectangle is 54 cm².
    The length of the rectangle is 9 cm.
    Find the perimeter of the rectangle.

22. Mrs. Jensen bought 4.5 ft of lace.
    She used 0.9 ft to make a dress.
    She used the rest to make 5 cushions of the same kind.
    Find the length of lace she used to make each cushion.

---

23. After spending $\frac{3}{5}$ of his money on a tennis racket, Sean had $14 left.
    How much did the tennis racket cost?

REVIEW 7

Write the answers in the boxes.

1. Write the missing number in each of the following:

   (a) The digit **8** in **58,**270 stands for 8 × ⬚.

   (b) The digit **5** in 48.**52** stands for 5 × ⬚.

2. Write 4 tens 6 tenths as a decimal. ⬚

3. What number is 0.1 more than 5.9? ⬚

4. (a) Write down **all** the factors of 20.

   ⬚

   (b) Write down **all** the common factors of 12 and 16.

   ⬚

5. Estimate the sum of 3548, 497 and 9621 by first rounding off each number to the nearest hundred. ⬚

6. Round off 147.25 lb to 1 decimal place. ⬚

7. Which one of the following is the greatest?

   4.2, 4.3, 4.23, 4.32 ⬚

8. Which one of the following is the smallest?

   $\dfrac{5}{4}, \dfrac{1}{2}, \dfrac{3}{4}, \dfrac{3}{8}$ ⬚

9. Which one of the following is the same as $1\dfrac{1}{2}$?

   1.1, 1.2, 1.5, 2.2 ⬚

10. Write the missing number in each of the following:

(a) 385 ml × 4 is equal to [ ] ℓ [ ] ml.

(b) 3 km 650 m is equal to [ ] m.

11. The amount of water in the jug can fill 3 glasses.
What is the capacity of each glass?

[ ]

12. Mr. Morrison made 6 plant holders.
He used 3.82 m of wire for each plant holder.
How many meters of wire did he use altogether?

[ ]

13. Casey cut a wire 8 ft long into 6 equal pieces.
How many feet long is each piece?
(Give the answer correct to 1 decimal place.)

[ ]

14.

Shrimps	$1.50 per 100 g
Fish	$4.50 per kg

Mrs. Goldberg bought 500 g of shrimps and 1 kg of fish.
How much did she spend altogether?

[ ]

15. John had $1.50.
He bought a ruler for 50 cents.
What fraction of the money did he have left?

[ ]

16. Karen earned $840 a month.

She spent $\frac{2}{5}$ of it on food.
How much did she spend on food?

[ ]

17. Gene walked 5 times around a rectangular field measuring 45 yd by 20 yd.
    How many yards did he walk altogether?

18. How many of the marked angles are right angles?

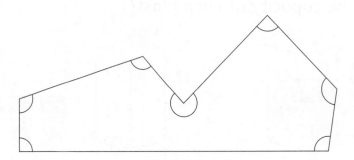

19. The figure shows a solid that is made up of 1-cm cubes.
    What is the volume of the solid?

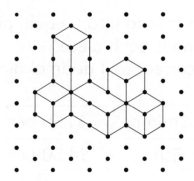

20. A tank measures 15 m by 6 m by 5 m.
    It is filled with water to a depth of 4 m.
    How much water is there in the tank?
    Give the answer in cubic meters.

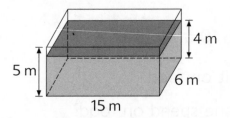

21. A picture measures 30 cm by 24 cm.
It is mounted on a rectangular card leaving a margin of 3 cm around it.
Find the perimeter of the card.

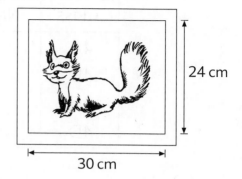

24 cm

30 cm

22. Ali used $\frac{3}{4}$ of his money to buy a watch which cost $45.
How much money did he have left?

23. The table shows the number of 4th grade students wearing glasses.

Class	No. of students wearing glasses
4A	6
4B	14
4C	10
4D	4

(a) How many students wear glasses?
(b) Use the data given in the table to complete the bar graph below.

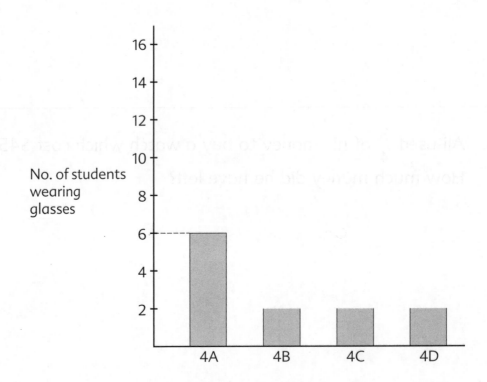

24. A tank can hold 30.1 gal of water.

A bucket can hold $\frac{1}{7}$ as much water as the tank.

Find the capacity of the bucket.

---

25. The perimeter of a rectangle is 30 in.
The width of the rectangle is half the length.
Find the area of the rectangle.

26. John saved 15 quarters in January.
    He saved 35 nickels in February.
    He saved 21 dimes in March.
    How much money did he save in the three months?

_____

27. How many quarters are there in $116.75?